Welcome to Holly Cottage

Welcome to Holly Cottage

NORMA COLLIS

IGUANA

Copyright © 2021 Norma Collis
Published by Iguana Books
720 Bathurst Street, Suite 303
Toronto, ON M5S 2R4

All rights reserved. No part of this publication may be reproduced, stored in a retrieval system or transmitted, in any form or by any means, electronic, mechanical, recording or otherwise (except brief passages for purposes of review) without the prior permission of the author.

Publisher: Meghan Behse
Editor: Paula Chiarcos
Front cover design: Ruth Dwight, designplayground.ca

ISBN 978-1-77180-542-1 (paperback)
ISBN 978-1-77180-543-8 (epub)

This is an original print edition of *Welcome to Holly Cottage.*

To my late sister Laura, a constant advocate of every project we have ever taken on.

Foreword

While many people dream of owning and operating a Bed and Breakfast, few of us are lucky enough to see that dream come true.

Over the years, many people have asked us where the idea to open a B&B came from. Likewise, they've asked us to share some of the "behind-the-scenes" experiences and insider knowledge we've gained throughout the ever-changing and intriguing journey that our Bed and Breakfast business has taken us on.

Welcome to Holly Cottage.

Chapter 1

This Sounds Like a Good Idea

My husband and I first discovered and promptly fell in love with B&Bs during a trip to England in the 1980s. I had just completed a university degree while holding down a full-time teaching job. As you can imagine, things got quite stressful at times, but it was the promise of a celebratory post-graduation trip to England that got me through the most discouraging moments in my pursuit of higher education.

Visiting England had been a long-standing desire of mine. After experiencing the relief and the satisfaction of receiving my cap and gown, we finally began to plan a two-week trip to England, which would be self-directed. We would rent a car and thoroughly explore the southern areas. We vowed to avoid using major motorways as much as possible and that we would stay exclusively in B&Bs tucked away in either rural areas or in small towns and villages.

When we told our Toronto-based travel agent what we planned to do as far as accommodations were concerned, she gasped in horror. "Oh no!" she said. "Lino floors, bad food, and lumpy beds? You won't like B&Bs! Let me book you into some nice hotels!"

But we followed our own instincts. Contrary to her expectations, some of our fondest memories associated with that trip involved knowledgeable hosts, cozy chats over cups of tea, and wonderful glimpses into the true nature of British homes. We experienced stays in a variety of delightful homes. The B&Bs included grand homes listed in the *Domesday Book*, along with one traditional Devon longhouse cottage. My husband, Dave, insisted later that the cottage had been designed for a family of Hobbits.

Indeed, the members of the host family were all quite small in stature and did look as if they'd fallen off a charm bracelet. During our stay, there were three children in the family who were in constant gales of laughter as they watched the two "North American giants" gingerly pick their way through the extremely low-beamed rooms. We could stand up only in the spaces between the beams. To get to our bedroom we had to navigate a very crooked, winding staircase, which we accomplished on our hands and knees, dragging our luggage behind us.

On subsequent trips abroad or even here in North America, we always included stays at local Bed and Breakfasts in our plans. The experiences afforded to us in these establishments allowed us a glimpse of the local lifestyle of each region in which we stayed.

Some of our most memorable side trips while staying at B&Bs were those recommended by our hosts. These weren't trips that you would normally find in a brochure or on a Things To Do in the Area website.

Many hosts suggested restaurants with the best meals in the area. These recommendations usually included quirky pubs and small family-run cafes that served locally sourced foods.

It was during one of our many Devon cream teas that we began to seriously discuss the possibility of running our own Bed and Breakfast. What started off as a joke between us gradually became a serious topic of conversation.

Over the next twenty years, we stayed in a wide variety of B&Bs. We talked to our hosts and found that many of them were very forthcoming about the pros and cons of the business.

From these conversations and experiences, we began to formulate a plan and an operational guide for our own business.

The "market research" we conducted throughout these stays provided us with a very clear understanding of how we wished to be treated as guests, which ultimately shaped how we intended to treat those who would visit our B&B. When talking to B&B owners, the overarching message was that, while we would never accumulate great wealth in the business, our lives would be forever enriched by the varied, highly interesting, and sometimes somewhat eccentric people who would cross our threshold. "You'll be on call 24/7," they warned. "You'll learn to power nap midafternoon if you're lucky enough to get a short break. You'll become very adept at changing breakfast menus at a moment's notice and at removing mystery stains on the run, while retaining a sense of humour at all times."

Additional pieces of advice covered such topics as returning forgotten articles to guests. "Do not do this, unless requested by the guest," they warned. They explained that not all guests may have been visiting you with their spouse. Their romantic tryst at your place of business may have been top secret. Can you imagine some unsuspecting spouse receiving a carefully wrapped skimpy and expensive piece of lingerie with a B&B business card attached to it? "Do you want to be responsible for the subsequent fallout from such a delivery?" we were asked. Our response: "No, we'd rather not."

They told us that some repeat guests may arrive with hostess gifts and send thank-you cards after their stay. This makes it hard to keep a balanced business head and to remember that, yes, you must still charge them because, after all, this is a business, and their stay has cost you money.

However, a plus they didn't tell us about occurred frequently once we opened our own business. We had several young couples who returned to stay with us time and time again. Their first visit would see them arrive in a small sports car, top down, travelling with one small case each. A year or two later, they would return as first-time parents. The sports car replaced by a more practical sedan. There would be slightly more luggage, even if they had left baby at home with the grandparents. Then, on the next visit, they would arrive in some sort of minivan. This time, there would be several young ones strapped into car seats and far more luggage, which meant trip after trip into the house carrying bags and various pieces of baby gear. Despite the extra hassle, it was quite heartwarming to see, and it meant that we became the honorary grandparents of several little ones. Sometimes, if we counted backwards, it was obvious that there had been a very romantic stay at Holly Cottage nine months prior to the birth of one of these youngsters. As we got to know our repeat guests better, we would rejoice with them over recently earned degrees, newly purchased homes, and freshly minted marriages. We also grieved with them over lost loves, alarming family illnesses, and heart-wrenching personal losses.

Even though we received some great advice prior to the outset of our journey, there were certain other things we learned as we went. We learned to keep our home "company ready" at all times and, consequently, not make personal plans too far in advance. This meant we celebrated major holidays before or after the actual date, depending on our ever-changing schedule. We also learned to always have our cell phone with us and to check the online reservation site frequently. Even with online reservations, many people wanted a follow-up phone call. They wanted to hear a real voice so that they could get a sense of who we were before staying in our home. We found if we didn't reply promptly, the guest would simply move on to the next B&B on the list.

Having to be constantly available like this made taking personal vacations problematic since, even during the shoulder seasons, people like to plan ahead.

Other owners may run their business in a different and more pragmatic way, choosing to simply close their doors for periods of time. However, once you take the "accommodating" out of the accommodation business, you run the risk of coming up short with more empty rooms than you had counted on.

We quickly concluded that if you have a true calling for the B&B business, you'll find ways to embrace and deal with all the inconsistencies and personal inconveniences related to the business. You'll do it because you love every moment of the adventure. And, if you're as lucky as we've been, you'll be left with a treasure trove of memories. Hopefully, you'll gather enough rich experiences to fill a manuscript.

You'll meet the most engaging people and amass endless anecdotes that arise from the wonderful guests who stay at your Bed and Breakfast. And, inevitably, there will be at least one memorable guest who will ask you at the end of every visit, "Am I still in chapter one in your B&B book?"

Chapter 2

In Search of the Perfect Place

To us, running a Bed and Breakfast seemed to be a perfect segue into full retirement. A venture such as this would keep us busy, allow us to meet new people, and perhaps even help us build up a retirement fund, considering that, for one of us, years of work didn't include any sort of pension plan.

Our search began well before the introduction of Google and virtual house tours. Whenever we spent time in Cottage Country, we scoured the windows of real estate offices looking for the newest postings of properties for sale. We read each new real estate guide from cover to cover and tried to view at least one property that might suit our needs whenever we were in the Lake Huron region of Ontario.

Having already renovated an older home (circa 1900) in the city of Brampton, we weren't afraid to take on another such project. I wasn't looking forward to dealing once again with the insidious nature of drywall dust and the inconvenience of nonexistent kitchen spaces awaiting a new look or having to use very sketchy bathrooms also awaiting a major facelift. Well, as they say ... "Needs must," "Stiff upper lip," and all those other old sayings that really just mean "Oh, get over it and get on with things!"

We quickly realized that our budget would not stretch enough to buy property in any of the lakeside communities where we'd spent our childhood summers. Even during times of economic recession, a nearby nuclear power facility in the area allowed people to earn high salaries and kept the price of properties well beyond our reach. We knew we'd have to pay for and maintain two properties for a good number of years. We'd continue to live in the community where we both worked while renovating our more northern enterprise. We looked at properties for over ten years and had offers fall through on two different places during that time.

One home was a large Arts and Crafts–style house in a small town inland from one of the lakeside communities that we knew well. It had originally been the home of the local veterinarian. There was a separate side entrance off an attractive wraparound porch, which would have given us a private entrance to our own living quarters. At the time, the home was owned by a local church and was being used as the minister's residence, otherwise known as a *manse*. The house was totally empty of furnishings because the church was awaiting the arrival of a new minister who preferred to purchase his own home. I knew from my own experience as a preacher's kid that more and more ministers were opting to purchase a home of their own.

This allowed them to build up equity they would need when they retired from the ministry and were faced with providing their own living arrangements.

The real estate agent certainly did his due diligence regarding the fact that the house had at some point been treated with urea formaldehyde insulation. Having had friends go through the same experience with their home, we knew what was involved with the removal of this dangerous product and the approximate cost to do it. We had to figure that cost into our offer price. We weren't in a hurry to take up residence there ourselves, so we offered to let the new minister live in the home rent-free for one year, as long as he paid for the utilities. This would give him an opportunity to look for a home to buy for himself. The offer then had to be presented to the church board. The agent told us we were offering "a sweet deal." He was, however, nervous about presenting the offer to this large group of individuals, some of whom had a reputation of being very tight-fisted. In the end, our offer was soundly turned down. The majority of the board members refused to accept the fact that the insulation in question had to be removed, even though the removal was required by law.

I was heartbroken. In my mind's eye, I had already redecorated that place, envisioning each piece of our antique furniture in the various rooms. For years after, I would, on occasion, have a recurring dream where we found ourselves living in that home.

Despite our disappointment over missing out on the manse, running Holly Cottage brought about many serendipitous moments. During the first spring that our business was open, we got a call from a woman who opened up the conversation by asking, "Are you open? I need to run away from home." I immediately imagined a very angry husband, fists raised, pounding on our front door in the middle of the night, with a loaded shotgun in the back seat of his vehicle. I must have given an audible gulp because she quickly added that her husband had found our listing in a local publication and suggested she take several quiet, calming days in a rural setting. I was able to collect myself enough to take down her details and assign her to a room. She enjoyed the solitude and the calming countryside views from our fireplace room and, by day two of her stay, began to tell us a little about herself. "I live in a small town near Lake Huron where my husband is a minister." Wait a minute, what did she just say? She named the town, and it was the same town where our former dream home was located. How much of a coincidence could this be? Through further discussion, it was quickly determined that it was, in fact, the same house and the same minister. "Well," she said, "my teenage daughter and I constantly clash. I'm running away from that but also from that terrible house!" She then proceeded to tell us about all the things that were wrong with the house. They were things that only a resident of the home would discover — things we had not picked up on during our viewing of the house. She told us that no other offers had come in on the house. As there was no sale, there were no housing allowance funds for the minister. She told us that from time to time one of the church board members would say, "I wonder whatever happened to that couple who put in the offer on the manse? Did they ever find a house? Would they still be interested in the manse?"

She said, "Now I have an ending for that story." I replied that now I, too, could lay those recurring dreams and feelings of regret to rest once and for all.

Of all the B&Bs in the area, how did she select our place? We decided that there really must be a higher authority in charge of the world.

When we did eventually purchase our 1878 stone farmhouse, we had no idea that this would lead us to an even more serendipitous experience in our lives.

Chapter 3

The Search Continues

After losing out on the manse, we licked our wounds for a year before resuming our search for a dwelling that would lend itself well to becoming a B&B home and business. At one point, we considered a renovated schoolhouse, but such places generally sit on very small pieces of property, and we knew we would have to build an addition to the existing building. Fortunately, the same real estate agent knew of another listing in the same general vicinity. It was a stone farmhouse that was being shared by several families from out of the area, who used it as a ski chalet during the winter months.

It took a bit of persuading on her part before the listing agents would relinquish the key so that she could show us the property. It wasn't her listing and she hinted that the agents were none too pleased to have a woman show one of their properties. They gave her absolutely no background information on the home.

As a child, I lived for nine years in a small Ontario town that contained a number of stone buildings. As such, I've always had an affinity for stone homes. My husband's strong Irish heritage led him to share this same deep respect and admiration for homes constructed of local stone. We could both see a great deal of potential in this particular house. The fact that it sat on two acres of land also meant that we might be able to add on to the existing building. At that time, an attractive board-and-batten family room had already been added to the original building.

We had realized that the owners were all lawyers, as law magazines had been strategically placed on every surface. We laughed when we saw these and remarked that "we had been warned." It was obvious that negotiating with this particular set of owners would not be easy.

We made the offer and waited to hear back from the sellers by an agreed-upon deadline. At the eleventh hour, our agent phoned us. She'd discovered that the stone structure had been gutted by a fire and then rebuilt. All our alarm bells went off. I have a fear of house fires and I was quite surprised at how much this particular piece of news upset me. "I don't think I can live there," I told the agent. She replied that she would feel exactly the same way. Again, we put our search on hold.

Some months later, I was casually flipping through a real estate guide, when a grainy black-and-white photo of another stone home caught my eye. As this home was located a good hour and a half north of the other, we decided it would be best to deal with the home's listing agent, who was located in Owen Sound. He spent a while on the phone with me, describing each room in detail. He then suggested that we meet at his office in Owen Sound. "You'll never find the place," he said. "It's located in the tiny hamlet of Woodford."

When I told this news to David he stopped for a moment and said, "Mom always called Woodford her hometown." My mother-in-law had passed away by this time, and I didn't remember ever hearing her say this. I put it out of my mind, and we really didn't give it much thought in the months that followed.

It was a cloudy day when we eventually looked at the house, which was completely empty of any furnishings, but I fell in love with the place the minute we walked in the door. As I told David later, "That house just seems to hug you." The deep pine-panelled windowsills just begged for plants, comfortable cushions, and a cat or two. Its wide-plank pine floors gleamed, and each room was spacious with high ceilings. The owners had started to renovate the place when their relationship fell apart. Having been through extensive house renovations before, we totally sympathized. They had removed walls both upstairs and down, which eliminated a lot of the dusty and dirty renovations that I wasn't anxious to experience again. The kitchen floor had been covered with large Mexican clay tiles. These were, of course, not original to the house but seemed to keep with the age of the home.

We learned later from neighbours that the kitchen had always been one very large room. They showed us where the cookstove had been placed and then regaled us with stories of one rather eccentric owner, who could often be found sitting in front of the stove with his feet resting on the open oven door. This same owner had at one time run a knife-and-saw-blade sharpening business in the enclosed front porch, and the porch had always been dirty and filled with oily rags. All of this got tracked into the large kitchen, where his poor wife had to deal with oil-smeared floors and countertops. Apparently, at one point, the two had a serious falling out. He moved out and onto the escarpment overlooking the house. He built himself a shack up there but made sure he was able to view the house to monitor his wife's comings and goings. Somehow, he managed to father six children in the midst of all of this marital discord.

The house was what can be categorized as a typical Ontario farmhouse. Above the upstairs hallway lancet-shaped window was a carefully carved keystone bearing the date 1878. It seemed very promising that a home of that vintage would have many stories to tell. We quickly purchased the place and happily began to use it as our weekend home.

Just down the road from the house was a small United church, where we began attending services. The other members of the congregation were welcoming, though very curious about us and how we would adjust to life in their hamlet.

David's mother had grown up on a farm in the area in what the locals still referred to as the "Irish Block." Some residents recalled going to school with her and her many brothers and sisters. The Irish Block was a Roman Catholic farming community comprised of Irish immigrants who arrived in the 1800s. There was an audible gasp from some of the good church folk when they first realized our family connection to the "Block." They stopped short of saying out loud what they were all obviously thinking:

What is an Irish Catholic boy doing attending a Protestant church? One of the older members, a true gentleman at all times, quickly spoke up. He said, "You know, David, your grandfather was a very open-minded man too. He sent your mother and all of your aunts and uncles to the little Protestant country schoolhouse in the area. He felt the Catholic school was too far away for his children to walk to in the winter." His statement immediately diffused the situation, and we all moved on to safer conversations about the weather and how various area crops were doing.

We'd been attending the church for about a year when a very elderly couple arrived at church one Sunday. They had farmed in the area for all of their working lives and had retired to a small home in Owen Sound. They only ventured out to their original church when the weather was favourable. "How do you like living in the old stone farmhouse?" the retired farmer asked us. I replied that I loved it and when I had time, I intended to search the history of the house.

"I know it must have a lot of stories to tell," I said.

He paused, gave me a very quizzical look, and said, "But you must know that your husband's grandparents lived in that house when they first immigrated here from Ireland? I thought that's why you bought it. I thought you wanted to get it back in the family." We were stunned. We had no idea that there was this kind of a family connection to the place.

There was no one remaining in my mother-in-law's immediate family who could fill us in on any details. We did know that she had married at quite a young age and that her first husband was a local who was significantly older than she was. He died of leukemia a year after they married. Her heart broken, she left the area. The Second World War had just begun, and she enlisted in the Women's Army Corp. She was sent to England and assigned the role of ambulance driver. She once told my sister-in-law that she took the most dangerous assignments handed out, as she really didn't care if she survived. She told this same sister-in-law a story about being sent to the south coast one dark night to pick up the wounded who were being shipped back to England by boat, under cover of darkness. The wounded included German military personnel as well as Allied fighters. The orderlies assisting in the receiving of the wounded were instructed to search any enemy patients carefully before loading them into the back of the ambulances. The stretchers were placed on bunks running along the sides of the vehicles. There was screen mesh separating the driver and co-driver, who rode in the front seat. One night, the searchers missed a stiletto knife a German soldier had hidden in his long knee socks. During the journey, he pulled the knife and stabbed and killed the co-driver, who was sitting right beside my mother-in-law.

After the war, my mother-in-law attended a dance in Toronto put on for all ex-military personnel. My father-in-law, being an ex-military member as well, attended. They met, fell in love, married, and had four children. My husband, David, was the oldest. In later years, she seldom spoke of the Irish Block. We knew the area still held painful memories of her first marriage.

I couldn't believe that all those years of searching for the perfect home would have led us in such a serendipitous route to this particular home in this particular area of Ontario.

I then understood why the house "hugged us" when we first walked through the front door. We were meant to live there. All of the other house-searching experiences we had gone through were just part of the road that led us to our real home at Holly Cottage.

Chapter 4

What's In a Name?

Over the years, many of our guests have asked us how we came up with the name Holly Cottage Bed and Breakfast. We explained that just after purchasing our stone farmhouse, I was subjected to a great deal of teasing and questioning as to whether we had made a wise purchase. These gentle and not-so-subtle comments came from my co-workers at the school where I taught. "What are you doing buying a place in the middle of nowhere?" they asked. "There's nothing to do there. You'll be so bored."

At the beginning of each school year, the staff always had a party on the weekend following the first week of school, which included a pig roast. I decided to throw down the gauntlet and asked the staff if they would be willing to make a drive north to our newly purchased weekend home for the annual party. Surprisingly, they all accepted. Since our home was located at the foot of the Niagara Escarpment, and the hamlet of Woodford sits on the top of the escarpment, we knew that a party of this size would not go unnoticed by the locals. Most of the inhabitants of the hamlet had a bird's eye view of our place.

We became acutely aware of this when we returned from a local auction with a car full of purchases. We had just carried in the last item when our phone rang. It was a lady from the village. "I recognized most of what you just carried into your house, but what was that last thing?" she asked. At that time, our landline was on a party line, and we could hear the ticking of the wall clock in another neighbour's kitchen. We knew that neighbour was listening in as well and that we were informing more than one inquiring mind, so we chose our words very carefully. Our purchases that day included a huge wooden barrel that came from a long-gone general store and was probably used to store flour. That was the item that had caught her eye and left her wondering what on earth we were going to do with it.

We decided that it would be best to invite all the inhabitants of the village as well as the teaching staff to the party. However, we were a little worried about how these two "different worlds" would get along. We had already been told by a local, jokingly we hoped, that "you can only live up on the rock if you're born in Woodford," so what would they make of all these outsiders?

Some of our closest teaching friends already knew of our intention to open a B&B. However, we hadn't as yet broadcasted this news to the locals. Change was often viewed with great skepticism tempered with a large dose of negativity, and we decided to proceed with any public declaration of our future plans with great caution.

Our elderly neighbour across the road from us was the proud owner of an Overland Willys-Knight antique car, which sported wooden wheel spokes and a wooden steering wheel. He immediately volunteered to provide scenic rides for our guests. The guy drove like a speed demon, but we figured he would be a big hit with our city guests. Hours before the party, he showed up in our front yard and inquired, "Are they here yet?" This happened numerous times. Previously, we'd wondered if there was some sort of hidden tunnel from his property to ours, as he frequently popped up in our front yard at the most unlikely times.

The day of the party he arrived with the car bedecked with colourful balloons. He parked at the very end of our driveway, as close to the main road as he could get. He wanted to make sure that no one missed this party destination. Everyone did find us, and they had a fantastic time. The hair-raising joyrides were a huge hit. Weeks later, those unforgettable rides were still the main topic of discussion in the school staff room.

Many of our guests, both visiting and local, arrived with guitars, and so the evening finished up with music and laughter around a large campfire. Many bottles of wine washed away any prejudices or uncertainties, and the guests mixed and mingled as if they'd known each other for years. I should also add that several of the village bachelors were quick to spot the single city ladies in the group.

At some point in the late hours of the evening, one of my co-workers mentioned our B&B plans. There was a momentary pause. Then one of the locals asked, "So what are you going to call the place?" When we replied that we didn't have a name yet, someone else suggested that the party guests all brainstorm possible names. Of course, teachers always have pencil and paper at the ready. Frankly, I was surprised that the printing wasn't done on chart paper with various coloured markers.

At the end of the session, we were handed three full sheets of possible names. All of them were quite appropriate, but the name that stuck out was the one suggested by my sister, Laura. On either side of the front door of our new home, some very healthy-looking holly bushes were growing in much splendour. "I think you should call the place Holly Cottage," she said. Everyone else agreed and this was followed by an appropriate toast.

The die was cast, so to speak. We had declared our intentions. We had a name for the business. The pressure was on. No more chit-chat about the project. It was time to get serious.

Chapter 5

It's All about the Name

There are always some hurdles to jump when solidifying a name for a business. Our first problem was that there was already a Holly Cottage Bed and Breakfast located in the south of England. Since they had registered that name on the internet, we had to be creative when registering our own website name. After numerous attempts, we finally settled on putting the first letter of our last name at the beginning of Hollycottage, creating an address that began with Chollycottage. This caused some difficulties with guests using only "Holly Cottage" as a search term. The name, however, did bring us a number of guests from the British Isles. Many of them told us that the name of our B&B gave them the sense they were booking into a place that would feel like home and they hoped we knew how to make a proper cup of tea. Thanks to my grandmother, I'd been properly schooled in the intricacies of heating the pot first and other details necessary to brewing a very acceptable "cuppa."

That Christmas, our gift from my sister, who had named the business, turned out to be a complete set of china with the logo Holly Cottage printed on a gate leading to an English garden in front of a very English cottage. We were thrilled and assumed that, somehow, she had commissioned someone to create the design. We were astonished to realize that the design was a registered pattern with a pottery company located in England. A friend of hers had been browsing in a china shop in Stratford, Ontario, when she stumbled upon the Holly Cottage set of china and immediately phoned my sister. "Do David and Norma know about this china pattern?" she asked.

"I don't think so," replied my sister. "But I know what they're getting for Christmas."

We had a number of sets of china to use for our breakfast guests. We always referred to the Holly Cottage set as our "How wide awake is the guest?" pattern. We generally plated the food in the kitchen and served breakfast in that manner. Some guests would sleepily shovel in their food until they got down to the pattern on the plate and not notice a thing. Other times we would hear someone say, "Wow. This says Holly Cottage. I wonder how they did that?" The teenagers who helped us out during our busiest months were always very relieved when this was the china of the day because it was the only set that could go into the dishwasher.

Given our business name, when guests would phone to make inquiries, they would often begin the conversation by saying, "Hello, Holly?" Most of the time, it was easier to just let on that Holly was my name and let the conversation roll on from there.

When a new neighbour purchased a home down the road from us, the confusion surrounding my name became quite humorous. I should note that she had a very thick Hungarian accent, which made her mistake all the more endearing. She often needed advice as to the management of the mechanical needs of her new home. I would answer the phone and she would always begin the conversation with "Hello, Holly?" After calling me this for almost a year she mentioned to another neighbour that Holly and her husband were very helpful with the running of her home. To which the neighbour responded: "Holly? There isn't anyone with that name in the area that I know of." The poor mistaken lady phoned our place, full of apologies. "I'm so, so sorry," she repeated over and over again. "All this time I thought your name was Holly. Why didn't you correct me?"

This neighbour's thick accent also led to what we now refer to as "the case of the purloined poop." It all began one November day when we headed into the city to purchase many of the products we needed to run the business. At that time, my husband owned a large lawn tractor that could be converted to a snow blower in the winter. It was at the George C. South dealership undergoing its winter maintenance and ready to be returned to us. We asked if they would mind holding off for a day or so, given that we weren't comfortable with a piece of machinery sitting out with the key in the ignition while we were away.

We returned home at dusk. In the light snow covering everything, we could see that a large vehicle had driven down our driveway. We assumed there had been a mix-up and the dealership had returned the tractor. Except there was no tractor parked by the garage or anywhere else on the property. It was then that we noticed there were other strange markings in the snow that went around the front of the house, down the yard, and back to our septic bed. With the help of a powerful flashlight, we determined that someone had dug out the access lids to our very large septic holding tanks. We were flabbergasted. Who would do such a thing?

We searched all around the front door to see if any note had been left and found nothing. It was then that David thought to phone the neighbour directly across the road to see if they had noticed anything strange happening at our place that day. He said that his wife thought she had seen a large truck in our yard and she assumed that we were having our septic pumped. We learned the name of the company and first thing the next morning called them. They knew nothing about making a call at our place.

The neighbour phoned again to see if we had learned anything about our mysterious visitors. "I think you had better call the police," he advised.

"When they ask us what seems to be missing, what will I say?" I replied. Immediately I had this vision of replying to the investigating officer, "What's missing? Well, we have no shit." Quite literally "No poop." We seem to have been the victims of a drive-by septic tank theft.

Later that morning the woman with the heavy accent phoned, very upset. "You won't believe what happened," she said. "I arranged for a company to come and pump out my septic tank. They never showed up and then had the nerve to call and tell me what the charges were. They also told me that the tank is huge and I know that's not true."

Well. Case solved. We immediately phoned the correct septic company. Our neighbour had told the company that she lived past Holly Cottage Bed and Breakfast. All the dispatcher could make out was "Holly Cottage."

When we finally solved the mystery of the purloined poop, everyone involved thought it was hysterically funny except for our poor neighbour, who still had a septic very much in need of attention.

Another problem we had not anticipated was with the inclusion of the word *cottage* in our name. As we lived in Cottage Country our business name would come up whenever someone would do a search by Googling "cottage/Meaford." We received hundreds of phone requests from folks who assumed we were renting out a lakeside cottage. This became problematic particularly if English was a second language for the person making the inquiry. We would try to very carefully explain the situation, sometimes with success and sometimes leaving the person who made the inquiry in a state of complete confusion. We eventually contacted a local cottage-rental agency and got their permission to give out their contact information.

Chapter 6

Reverend Jerry

We were still working on the interior of the large new wing we added to our 1878 farmhouse, when four administrators from a Bible camp just down the road arrived at our front door. "We understand you're preparing your place to be a Bed and Breakfast. How soon can you have it open?" they asked. This shocked us into finishing the project in a timely manner. If not for that visit, we would have likely been fine-tuning and humming and hawing for quite some time before we found the courage to hang out our sign and officially open our doors.

One of our first set of guests was Reverend Jerry, his gracious wife, and a young married couple, all from Defiance, Ohio. They had travelled for hours with several vehicles full of energetic teens eagerly awaiting their summer experience at the Bible camp. Rev. Jerry was a rather rotund gentleman and quite impressive in manner. The fact that he spoke with a slight Southern drawl merely added to his overall charm. The first night that they stayed with us, they retired to bed very early because everyone was exhausted from the long car trip. Sometime during the night Rev. Jerry awakened to find that he'd forgotten to remove his contact lenses before heading to bed, and one lens was now sitting on his cheek. His lens case and wetting solution were still out in his car, so he crept down the stairs and unlocked the front door. Our front door actually had two locks. One was situated right in the door handle and we seldom used it. Rev. Jerry didn't know this, of course, and he proceeded to set the lock in the door handle instead of leaving it in the unlock position.

"There I was," he told us the next morning, "middle of the night, wearing my bright-green pyjamas and locked out of the house."

His wife had suddenly awakened and realized that he was missing. As he had recently had a knee replaced, she was concerned that the knee might have given out somewhere in the house. "There I was," she told us, "tiptoeing through your house and whispering Jerry's name as loudly as I dared." It was then that she looked out of the French doors in our dining room. "There he was," she said, "striding along the side of your home, looking up toward the sky."

"Were you looking for divine intervention?" I asked.

"No," he replied. "I had a handful of gravel from your driveway and I was trying to figure out which upstairs window I should throw some pebbles at to wake up my wife."

We all laughed at the picture he must have presented to anyone driving by at that early time of day. A very rotund gentleman, sporting a big red beard and clad in bright-green pyjamas, resolutely walking the outside perimeter of the B&B. This sight would most certainly have elicited a second look from anyone passing by.

Jerry and his entourage stayed with us for a number of summers after that. At the end of each stay he would ask, "Well, am I still in chapter one of your Bed and Breakfast book?" I hope he'll be understanding of his placement in chapter six, although his story has been retold many times.

There is actually a part A to this story. A week before the big lock-out affair, we received a late-night phone call from a local restaurant with whom we often partnered when guests requested a special dining experience. The caller was the chef, who apologized profusely for phoning at eleven o'clock at night. "I have a couple of late-night diners here," he explained. "They're just now starting on the entrée and they don't have anywhere to stay for the night. May I send them to you?" My husband, ever the night owl, agreed that he would wait up for the midnight gourmands.

We also had a pair of honeymooners staying in the new section of the house. We decided it would be in everyone's best interest to have the new arrivals stay in the farmhouse wing because we didn't wish to disturb the newlyweds on their wedding night.

Just after midnight, David saw car lights coming down our driveway. *These will be the diners*, he thought. He was greeted at the front door by a very upset woman who informed him that she had just hit a deer out on the road. "It might still be alive. Can you go out and try to resuscitate it?"

Judging from the damage to the side of her car, David assured her that the poor animal was probably deceased and that his training didn't qualify him to carry out mouth-to-mouth on a deer. It took some persuading to get her to realize that the police needed to be called as she would need an accident report for her insurance claim. David got her seated in our front living room and brought her a glass of water. She seemed extremely nervous, and he realized that a strange man inviting her into his house at midnight might be a little disconcerting for a woman travelling alone in the countryside. Her distress was further enhanced by the fact that she was driving her daughter's car, which obviously did not now look like it had when she first borrowed it, après deer.

At that moment, more car lights came down the driveway. Out of a very small sports car leaped two extremely tall people. They explained that this was a very new relationship and they were being totally spontaneous about the time they spent together as they got to know each another better. We later speculated that they must have met at the Tall Persons' Club because he was almost seven feet tall and she stood at a good six and a half. It was quite obvious that they'd imbibed rather a lot during the course of their dinner and should not have been driving.

David tried to escort the talkative and rather hyper couple past the living room, where the highly distraught driver was seated, and up the steep stairs in the farmhouse to their designated bedroom. He assumed they would turn in for the night. To his dismay, they proceeded to explore the entire house, both inside and out. When he found them in the backyard toasting loudly with alcoholic coolers that they had brought with them, he had to get quite firm with the "spontaneous" couple.

When they realized the local constabulary were due to arrive at any moment and that the police might not share their drunken enthusiasm for young love, the couple finally retreated to their bedroom. It was then that David awoke me from a sound sleep. "Dead deer, drunken giants, police. If anything more happens, I'm out of here."

I got dressed quickly and made my way to the frightened car driver to assure her that there was also a woman in the house and that I wasn't inebriated like the other two people she'd seen speed past the living-room doorway.

The poor chef from the restaurant called to apologize the next morning. He'd driven past our place on his way home. "I saw a police cruiser in your yard, and then I saw a dead deer on the side of the road. Are those diners okay?"

We realized that anyone who passed by our place at the same late hour every weekend would have viewed a police car in our driveway on the first weekend and spied a large pyjama-clad man locked out of the place in the middle of the night on the next. To those with an imagination, it might appear that we had called the police to handle unruly guests one week and then the next week, simply locked another hard-to-manage guest out of the house.

This wasn't quite the business image we were hoping to project but it did provide material for a chapter in this book.

So yes, Rev. Jerry, you're definitely a central character in a two-part scenario that is now recorded in our Bed and Breakfast book.

Chapter 7

The Hookers Are Coming

When we first opened up our business, we were quite aware that the local people were very skeptical regarding our aspirations. Most were too polite to say so, but we could see the doubt clearly written on their faces. I'm sure we were the main topic of conversation at many a local gathering and I suspect there may have been a bet or two placed on when those two "naive" souls from the city would realize the folly of their ways. One local told us that people from "away" who settled in the area were referred to as *cityiots*.

After opening the business, we continued to attend the country church down the road from us whenever we could get away in time for the 11:30 a.m. service. Each Sunday we would see cars slowing down as people passed by on their way to church. We knew they were checking out our guest parking area to see how many cars were still there. We would see all the heads in each car turn and we knew what was happening. The church-goers were well aware that any cars remaining in the lot meant that we were still catering to guests and we would not be in attendance at church that day.

On the days that we were able to get to the service, someone would always ask, "How's business?" They were constantly amazed that people travelled to their little hamlet and actually paid money to stay in the area.

One Sunday during coffee hour, one gentleman asked my husband the usual question: "How's business?"

"Oh, not too bad," my husband replied. "Next week, we have a full house. The Hookers are coming for the week."

Coffee cups halted halfway to mouths and the proverbial pin could have been heard to fall. We had to hastily explain what was meant by this statement before risking permanent censure from our neighbours.

The Hookers were actually teachers who taught the old-fashioned techniques of rug hooking. Students of these artists were taught how to dye their own materials and design their own patterns in order to produce beautiful and authentic works of art. The teachers travelled to us from distant parts of Canada and the United States. They stayed with us in early March of each year and held their classes in several of the buildings at the church camp down the road.

The first year they stayed with us, one of the teachers travelled from South Carolina to teach about natural dyes and other homemade rugmaking techniques. Early spring in Grey County generally means grey skies, chilly temperatures, and snow-covered ground. This particular March was no exception. I offered to help carry in her belongings. She was happy with the offer as she had a carful of items. She handed me an armful of woollen blankets. I staggered under their weight and wondered to myself how these would be used in her teaching course. I knew that purist rug-hookers took used fabrics, cut them into strips, and wove the strips into eye-catching, three-dimensional designs. I thought perhaps the blankets were destined for such an activity.

I decided to ask her about the large quantity of blankets. She stopped what she was doing, gave me a "look," and then in a lovely Southern drawl replied, "Well, it is Canada, you know. Ah thought ah might be cold." We made sure she was given the Fireplace Room to stay in. She took full advantage of this feature. Each morning when I entered to make the bed and change the towels, a wall of heat rolled out to greet me. She had that gas fireplace cranked up to full capacity. It had to be at least 90 degrees Fahrenheit in there. The high temperature was maintained at that level for the duration of her stay.

She was a very gracious and charming woman, probably in her mid-seventies. Each morning she arrived at the breakfast table in a different outfit. Each ensemble had earrings and shoes to match. The last morning that they were with us, she arrived at the table sporting a large rhinestone brooch with the words *I'm a Hooker*. "Ah just love wearing this pin when ah go through customs," she told us.

The second year that the teachers stayed with us, a new teacher joined the group. She was somewhat quieter than the others and it wasn't until late in the week, at the encouragement of the others, that she showed us a rug of her own creation. It was a masterpiece. Her husband had recently died and it was created as a tribute to him. Her husband was a World War II veteran and an amputee.

Over their years together, she knitted him a variety of woollen socks to wear over the stump of his amputated leg. After his death, she carefully cut each sock into strips and then wove them into a rug. The scene depicted on the rug showed sheep in various colours grazing on a hillside. At the crest of the hill, and appearing to be on the verge of disappearing, was a shepherd. He wore a slouchy hat that covered his facial features. Rather than a crook, this shepherd travelled with the assistance of two crutches and he was missing his left leg. It was almost impossible for me to express my tearful thanks for what she had just shared with us. It was an intimate and personal insight into her very soul. There was no way to adequately express our gratitude for such a gift.

These same teachers presented us with a framed photo, which we hung on the wall just outside of the Fireplace Room. It shows a clothesline with pairs of brightly coloured long underwear pegged in place and blowing jauntily in the wind. One of the teachers had been given a large bundle of rather dingy and well-worn long underwear. "Here, you like fabrics. Perhaps you'll know what to do with these," she was told. She puzzled over the dubious usefulness of such a gift for a long time.

Eventually, she decided to open up a rug-hooking supply shop in her home. The shop was to be open on a by-chance basis. While wondering how she would let her customers know whether or not the shop was open, she was suddenly struck with the idea that she could put the dingy underwear to good use. She dyed each pair of long johns a vibrant hue until every colour of the rainbow was represented. Each time she opened up her shop, the eye-catching underwear was hung out on a clothesline that was clearly visible from the main road. This idea led to a series of prizewinning photos. We felt very privileged to be given a framed copy of one of these outstanding photos.

During their first stay with us, I mentioned that I wanted to someday write a book about our experiences at Holly Cottage. Each year upon their arrival, they would ask me how many more chapters I had added to the book since their last stay. "Tell us your newest stories," they would beg. Then they would sigh and add, "Oh, we're so boring. We'll never rate a chapter in your book."

After three years of repeating this disclaimer, something did happen that changed everything as far as the infamous Bed and Breakfast book was concerned.

One evening, after we all retired for the night, there was a minor traffic accident out on the main road. Someone hit black ice, spun out of control, and took out a portion of fencing before landing in a neighbour's field. One of our guests had awoken to emergency strobe lights reflecting off the ceiling in her bedroom. She watched the scene out her window as police, fire, ambulance, and then tow truck arrived. The rest of us slept blissfully through the entire event. The next morning at breakfast, she filled us all in on the midnight excitement.

That evening, my husband and I were attending a community meeting and our guests were attending a dinner party. They arrived home before we did. They were just settling in when the front doorbell rang. At first they thought it was the chiming of a clock. After a few minutes of discussion, they realized it was the doorbell and they made their way rather timidly to the front door to answer it. Standing outside was a very young and extremely good-looking police officer. He was investigating the property damages caused by the accident of the night before.

"Are you the owners of this home?" he inquired.

"Oh no, we're just the hoo—um ... er ... no ... we're guests?" they answered. Posing this statement as a question made their presence in the house even more questionable. They felt that only the fact that each one of them was old enough to be the young officer's grandmother saved them. That they were all garbed in various nightwear ensembles that were not at all "sexy" also may have saved us from further inquiries.

When we got home, they recounted this tale with great glee. "We almost became a chapter in your book," they announced. "Have you ever had to bail guests out of jail because they've just been charged with soliciting?"

Boring? I don't think so. Memorable? Absolutely. The Hookers have definitely rated a chapter in this book as well as our admiration and affection.

Chapter 8

Buying Locally

One Sunday during lunch after church, several of the local farmers were discussing the weather and the need for a stretch of dry days to allow for haying to take place. Quite innocently, David said, "Now you have to remember that I was brought up in a town. I've always wondered what the difference is between hay and straw." There was an audible gasp as sandwiches stopped partway to mouths. *Oh no*, I thought. *We haven't even been here for a year and we'll have to move.*

Our church family had a number of kind gentlemen who attended on a regular basis. One of these men quickly spoke up and explained the difference. "Hay is for eating and straw is used for bedding." This led to a very lively conversation about the fact that in tough times, straw could be wet down with sugar water and used for feed if hay was unavailable. This led to many of the older folks sharing their memories of how various relatives had resorted to this in order to feed stock during times of famine. Thankfully, this drew the attention away from us, for the moment.

A week or so later, we travelled down the sideroad to buy eggs from a local farmer who was a staunch member of our church. He was a formidable personage, small in stature but with a very stern and quite frightening countenance. His work hat was an ancient, battered fedora with a tired and floppy brim. He would peer up at you from under that brim in a totally terrifying manner. The farmer's wife was a sweet-mannered and always-smiling woman. Although they seemed like a very mismatched couple, they obviously adored each other. The walls of their farm kitchen were filled with photos of the many children they had fostered over the years. They continued to follow the lives of these children even as they reached adulthood and began to have families of their own.

A trip down the road for eggs meant clearing the calendar for the better part of the day, as the transaction would be a lengthy one. First we were invited to sit at the kitchen table while the farmer's wife served tea from a big Brown Betty teapot, along with a plate of freshly baked cookies. It was expected that we would be staying for an extended round of conversation and some "gentle" questioning as to the activities taking place at our own farmhouse.

It was during one of these roundtable discussions that the good farmer himself came in from the barn. He glowered at us from under the brim of his hat and then, turning to David, he said, "I'm taking you out to the barn and I'm going to show you the difference between hay and straw." He stopped short of saying *Then you'll never have to ask such a stupid question again.*

The "tour" lasted for over two hours. During that time, the farmer proudly showed off his barn, which his grandfather had built. The centre ridgepole running the length of the roof was constructed from a single tree and ran eighty-five feet. He recounted the tale of his grandfather felling the tree on the top of the escarpment and then the dangerous process of dragging it down the steep slope of the scarp. They used horses to do the heavy part of the work. He said that the horses' hooves kept slipping out from underneath them as they crept down the dangerous slope. Other people worked to stop the log from passing the horses and dragging them all down the slope after the runaway log. Over the years, many an area farmer has lost their life trying to control a tractor pulling a full wagonload down those slopes.

We fully believed his story, as quite recently, one very sad Thanksgiving weekend, such a tragedy had taken place during a holiday hayride. The ride included driving the wagon, loaded with people, down the steep slope of the Niagara Escarpment. One of the families involved was staying with us and survived the accident, sustaining only bumps and bruises. The driver was not so fortunate. In an act of heroism, he turned the tractor sideways to try to stop the wagon from sliding. This action caused the tractor to roll over, leading to the most tragic ending imaginable.

David's farm tour with the old farmer continued with a look at various pieces of antiquated farm machinery and horse equipment once used with the Clydesdale horses. At the end of the tour, he looked at David sadly and said, "You know, we weren't able to have children. We have no one to leave the farm to and it's been in our family for over one hundred years."

As a young man, he permanently damaged his lungs rescuing horses from a barn fire. Several years after this tour of his farm, he died from an asthma attack. His grieving wife then sold the farm and tried to make a new life for herself in town.

Shortly after her move into a town apartment, she herself passed away. I think she died of a broken heart. She quite literally pined away, missing her beloved husband and their cherished farm. The farm is now the site of a successful organic meat-and-produce business. Co-op students from all over the world come and live there. They actively work on the land while they learn about the newest growing techniques. The farm and the farmhouse are all lovingly cared for. I can easily imagine the old farmer and his wife holding hands and looking down from above. He is still wearing his beat-up old hat. If you peer closely under that floppy brim, he's smiling.

These two remarkable people taught us that good neighbours are all part of the rich tapestry of life. Such neighbours will be interested in your guests and your guests will be very interested in hearing stories about them. We tell these stories with great respect and with much admiration for these people who exemplified the phrase "salt of the earth."

Chapter 9

Local Lore

There are many more stories about the fierce but gentle farmer down the road. He was as thrifty as he was resourceful. His "new" car, which he drove to church on Sunday and into town from time to time, was at least fifteen years old. He always bought the same make and model of car, and as each vehicle reached the end of its road worthiness, it was assigned a permanent parking spot behind the barn. When the "new" car needed parts, he simply visited the site for superannuated autos behind the barn and removed the part needed to keep his current vehicle on the road.

Of equal vintage was his very ancient Oliver tractor. He had purchased this at a farm auction held at a local apple orchard. This style of tractor is designed to move between the apple trees. The exceptionally high side fenders on the vehicle allow it to drive past the trees without actually touching any and thereby damaging them. As our farmer friend was such a small man, he was almost invisible behind the large steering wheel and the oversized fenders. Seeing the tractor make its way down the road gave one pause to consider whether this was some sort of remote-control vehicle. Every once in a while you might catch a glimpse of a very battered and very old fedora making its way along the road atop an ancient tractor.

During the infamous hay-versus-straw tour, the farmer had shown David his prize chickens and explained that he was having a great deal of difficulty with raccoons getting into the chicken feed. One day after church, David asked him if he had solved the raccoon problem. The farmer proceeded to tell David about his misadventures with an entire family of raccoons. He decided that he would trap the animals and relocate them. The live trap was, of course, one of his own creation, built from leftover bits and pieces found around the farm. One by one, he managed to capture four baby raccoons and finally the mama herself. He carefully placed the large trap on the back of his Oliver tractor and started off with the intention of taking the raccoons on a "family" outing down country before releasing them. Just as he left his own driveway, he hit a large pothole. This collision between ancient vehicle and untended driveway caused the door of the trap to fly open. The farmer was unaware of this newest turn of events.

As he continued down the road, he suddenly realized that two baby raccoons were perched on one of the very large side fenders of the tractor. They were hanging on for dear life but seemed to be enjoying the ride. Then he looked over at the other side fender and there was the mother raccoon. She was also hanging on for dear life but not about to abandon her brood of babies. He stopped the tractor right in front of his neighbour's field. The entire family immediately jumped ship and ran off into a huge field of corn.

Later in the week, the farmer who owned the cornfield was talking to David. "I can't believe what my neighbour just did," he exclaimed. "That old bugger loaded up a family of raccoons, drove down the road on his tractor, and stopped to let them off right into my field of corn. He's lost it."

I've already mentioned the very steep and rocky terrain that makes up the Niagara Escarpment in the area where we lived. One of the locals, knowing my interest in local history, told me about a Baptist preacher who was a circuit rider. Back in the late 1800s, there were two area Baptist churches that shared the same preacher. One of the churches was located on the other side of a wetland that ran up to the base of the escarpment. The other church was located in the hamlet of Woodford, "up on the rock" as the locals referred to the village location. Each Sunday, weather permitting, this poor man of the cloth carried out a morning service at the lower church. He then proceeded to the steep and slippery slope of the escarpment, where he would begin to climb up. He then made his way through a thickly wooded area before beginning to climb again in order to reach the Woodford Baptist Church, where he would carry out his second church service of the day.

I would often tell that story to our hikers after they had completed that portion of the Bruce Trail. They would gasp and then tell us how difficult that portion of the trail was, even when they'd followed a cleared path with ropes in place to assist them over some of the most dangerous sections.

Some of the citizens of the hamlet of Woodford had their own regional dialect, which made for some very interesting if not confusing situations. One elderly lady would come out of her house and speak to me whenever I walked by. She would tell me long accounts of something she felt I should know about. I didn't understand one word she said. Her dialect plus a set of poorly fitting dentures put me in a very awkward position. I would nod or shake my head at what I hoped was the appropriate pause in the conversation. I could well imagine her telling her family that the new lady in the old farmhouse seemed friendly enough but, she feared, she wasn't very bright.

Another man in the village knew that David was an avid fisherman. He carefully explained where David would find an inland lake that was particularly good for fishing. "You go along the highway and then turn left at Josie's house," he said. Now we didn't want to admit that we didn't know who Josie was. We hoped we could figure this out for ourselves. We drove slowly along the highway as I stuck my head out through the open window trying to read mailbox names. We could not find a single Josie or anyone with the initial J on either side of the highway.

A few days later, we encountered the same man, who inquired if David had gotten out fishing at the spot that he'd recommended. We had to admit that we were completely stumped as to where we were supposed to turn. He looked at us as if we were two very unintelligent people. Then, very slowly and with great care, he explained that we were to turn left at the farm implement dealership called George C. South. "Ah," we said. "Of course, Josie's house."

We used that story and that reference point whenever we needed to direct guests in that same direction. They would return to the house later and tell us with great pride that they had turned left at "Josie's house" and that they'd reached their destination successfully. These are points of reference that even the most sophisticated GPS is not privy to. I have yet to meet a GPS that provides one with a good old-fashioned belly laugh.

Chapter 10

Good Neighbours

Our area of Southern Georgian Bay experiences extremely fierce snowstorms leading to phenomenal accumulations of snow. The hamlet of Woodford sits at a very high altitude and, consequently, snow-laden winds sweeping in off Georgian Bay hit that particular piece of high escarpment and drop their load of frozen precipitation right onto Woodford.

We learned to keep an emergency stock of tinned food in our pantry and mastered a whole new set of winter-driving skills. Snow tires went on the car in early October and weren't removed until the end of May. If one did become stuck in a snowdrift or was suddenly introduced to a country ditch, no one ever passed you by. People know that leaving you there could very well mean that they were leaving you in a life-or-death situation. Most people travel with chains in their car trunk and are very well-versed in the fine art of pulling a vehicle out of a very sticky situation. These good Samaritans won't accept money for their efforts and will shrug off any words of praise.

We had a guest get stuck at the end of our driveway one snowy afternoon. David was away at a meeting, so it was up to me to help her dig, push, and finagle her car back onto the main road. We struggled with the vehicle and achieved nothing despite our efforts. Suddenly, out of seemingly nowhere, two pickup trucks pulled up and four young men jumped out of them. The very fit fellows picked up her small car and set it down on the main road. Their task completed, they disappeared just as quickly as they had arrived.

"Oh, I'm so embarrassed," she said.

"Don't be," I replied. "They saw we were in trouble and they did what needed to be done. That's how it works around here."

One early piece of advice we carefully followed was offered to us shortly after purchasing our country home: "Don't say anything derogatory about one local person to another local. Chances are they'll be related." These were certainly words to live by. We had read about six degrees of separation. There were actually only two degrees in our "neck of the woods."

A very dear friend, who wasn't from the area originally, is well known for the very admirable trait of being very inclusive. She makes a point of introducing people to each other no matter what social situation she may be in. She laughingly told us about one occasion where her devotion to inclusivity really backfired on her. She was acting as an usher one Sunday morning at a local church. As she seated a couple in one of the pews, she took the time to introduce them to the other couple already seated in the same pew. All four people burst out laughing as she had just introduced a brother to his sister.

She said to us, "I should have known."

Then we all said in unison, "Two degrees of separation."

As I mentioned earlier, we decided not to tell the locals about our Bed and Breakfast plans until the time seemed right to do so. Change does not come easily to the area, and we wanted people to get to know us a little better before we hit them with our proposal. When we did finally "tip our hand" as to our plans, one local gentleman paused, seemed to give the news some consideration, and then said, "Well now, Woodford used to have accommodations back in the horse-and-buggy days; I guess it's okay if there are accommodations here again."

Indeed, at one time, Woodford boasted not one but three hotels. Local topography creates a steady uphill climb from Owen Sound to the summit of the escarpment and the hamlet of Woodford. It is an equally steep climb from the other direction if one is travelling from the town of Meaford. In the horse-and-buggy days, the horses pulling the stagecoach or cartage wagons had to be changed by the time they reached Woodford due to the extreme physical effort needed to reach the highest point of their trip, which was Woodford.

One hotel, located on the outskirts of the hamlet, was the "dry" hotel. At one time, there had been a large Quaker settlement in the immediate area. The choice of non-alcoholic accommodations seems quite logical. Along a local sideroad are the crumbling remains of the Woodford Quaker cemetery. Some faintly etched surnames can still be made out on the plain white tombstones. They bear the last names of some of the families whose descendants still live in the area.

If a traveller desired more powerful libations, they would disembark at the Woodford Hotel, located in the hamlet proper. This very large redbrick structure still stands in the village. It's now a private home. The present owners, when renovating, discovered that the former "ladies' drinking parlour," located to the left of the front entrance, remained in pristine condition. However, the gentlemen's bar, to the right of the front door, showed lasting evidence of many a drunken brawl. The wainscoting on the walls and the wide plank floors showed deep scratches and dents; lasting scars from a tougher and more expressive time, where flying furniture and fist-to-fist combat were a frequent occurrence.

The locals told us that, in a large, empty field directly across from our home, there sat a third hotel. This was a more upscale hotel and, of course, the rooms were more costly. This piece of land is now owned by the Bruce Trail Conservancy. Each spring, random bunches of daffodils still grow where, I imagine, the hotel's formal gardens might have been located. I can picture those more subdued travellers sitting on a broad veranda, sipping a sherry while waiting to be shown to their private and well-appointed bedrooms.

Since we knew very little of David's grandparents' history and their connection to Woodford itself, we were happy to have the use of a history book of the area that had been compiled and written by the local women's institute in the early 1900s. An elderly woman who was "the local historian" put this book in our hands and also filled us in on her own knowledge of our farmhouse and its connection to David's maternal grandparents. A late eighteenth-century local census listed David's grandfather as a hostelry man. We had to look that one up. We learned that title is given to someone who handles and takes care of horses. The job was often associated with livery stables and hotels. We don't know which hotel he may have worked at, but he did have the three to choose from. His other job was as the rural route #3 mail-delivery person. He collected the mail from the Woodford post office, then he rode his horse to Bognor, a small village south of Woodford. There he handed off the mail to a gentleman who would proceed to deliver all the Bognor-area mail.

Back in the day, Woodford was a thriving business hub, handling the Royal Mail post office, located in Woodford, added to the importance of the village. The original Woodford postmaster's desk now resides in a museum in Ottawa. It's a magnificent piece of elaborately carved furniture, probably ten feet in height, which has led us to speculate that it may have resided in the old hotel in the main part of the hamlet. The soaring ceilings in that structure would have easily accommodated such a large and magnificent piece.

Looking back through old documents housed in the country archives, we could find no evidence that David's grandparents every actually owned our 1878 farmhouse. We can only speculate that they resided there as renters until they'd accumulated enough cash to purchase what was to become the family farm in the Irish Block.

Once our own business was up and running, we would encounter various neighbours while we were out running errands. They continued to be astonished that anyone would travel to their little hamlet and would actually want to stay for several nights. Our neighbours would ask "Where do these people come from? What are they doing here? How long will they be staying?" We didn't look upon these queries as snoopiness but rather, as genuine curiosity. Perhaps over the years the locals had come to take the sheer beauty and uniqueness of their natural environment for granted. They didn't recognize how this setting would resonate in the souls of those who didn't live surrounded by such wonders.

Partway up the escarpment, at the mouth of the hamlet, sat the home of a long-time resident who referred to himself as the "mayor of Woodford." His wife had passed away several years before we moved to the area, so we didn't have an opportunity to meet her. Other people always spoke very highly of her. It was obvious that "the mayor" was a very lonely man. Every time he saw us, he would ask, "Have you met any nice single ladies who might want to go to Florida with me this winter?" We would laughingly reply that we really couldn't help him out, because we weren't "that sort of establishment." Several years after we opened our business, he had a large number of beautiful shade trees removed from his property. David asked him why and he replied, "Oh, I just wanted to have a better view of the intersection by your place." We suspected that the real reason for this creative forestry project was because he wanted to be able to observe the comings and goings up and down our driveway plus have an unobstructed view of our guest parking area.

One weekend, we had five sisters stay with us for a "girls' weekend" away. These "girls" were all quite mature with not one of them qualifying for the "under 70" club.

They were a very lively group and constantly on the go. They went on day trips, shopping trips, and were definitely part of the "ladies-who-lunch" set. Having been raised on a farm not far from where my father was raised, they were well aware of the highly interesting people who live in rural areas. They begged us to tell them about our rural neighbours. The "mayor of Woodford" was part of that conversation. I told them I was sure that he would be taking note of all of their comings and goings and would be very curious about them. I asked if any of them had any interest in travelling to Florida that winter. They all thought this was uproariously funny, with each sister nominating one of her siblings for that particular honour. After hearing the story, they blew kisses in the direction of his home whenever they left the B&B.

Sunday morning, we received a phone call from the "mayor."

"Who are those women staying at your place?" he asked. "Are any of them single? Would one of them like a free trip to Florida?"

Our guests were beside themselves when we gave them this news. They were delighted to think that someone would be inquiring about them at their age. "Did you tell him all five of us would be interested?" asked one of the sisters. This was followed by shrieks of laughter, and the sister who made the inquiry immediately had one of our home-baked muffins lobbed at her head by another sister.

This is the perfect example of one of the cardinal rules when running a B&B: Protect your guests at all costs. However, it is also a good idea to inform them of their "options."

Chapter 11

Behold the Unexpected

When running a B&B, you must be ready for the unexpected at all times.

When people tell us that they think they'd like to run a Bed and Breakfast, the first thing they ask is, "What are the most important things I should know about the business?" We tell them, "You must always be company ready."

It's not unusual to have someone knock on your front door and ask to see your rooms as they are booking rooms for a family wedding or an event that could be up to two years in the future. They may be looking for a wedding ceremony site or a place for the bride and her attendants to spend the night prior to the wedding day. This means they'll also expect to use your place as a venue for dressing, makeup, and even professional hair styling on the big day itself. You can also expect a photographer will be recording every step of the pre-ceremony preparation.

People are very excited about the impending big day and will consider it quite appropriate to show up at the door at 9:00 a.m. while you're "mid-breakfast service." The fact that you've arrived at the front door with a spatula in one hand won't faze them at all.

It's prudent to plan for these occurrences. We had a hard-and-fast rule that, no matter what the time of day, we wouldn't ever show a room if a guest was still using it. The guest might be out for the day, but their belongings were still in the room and because they paid for that room, it would be their private place of residence until they officially checked out. We would refer the inquiries to our website, which showed detailed photos of each room plus common areas. We'd offer to make an appointment for a more suitable time to meet with the perspective wedding party. After several wedding party experiences, we learned to be very careful, and very specific, about any "extras" we were prepared to offer and what the costs for these extras would be.

Most people were very understanding of the need to make an appointment for this discussion. We encountered a few who felt that their wedding plans should be discussed immediately upon their unexpected arrival. They felt this should take priority over everything else and anyone else who might be a guest at your place of business at that time. If people are overly demanding and somewhat unreasonable during their initial visit, you're most likely headed into a great deal of stress as you deal more with this group of individuals.

We quickly learned if you want to attract wedding business, be patient but do charge for all the extras that you're asked to provide. This may include appetizers or even a meal for the bride and her entourage for their bachelorette party on the evening before the wedding. There will most likely be a great deal of giggling and noise far into the night. It would be impossible to have other guests (not attached to the wedding) stay in the house at the same time. This means a loss of income if the bridal party does not rent the entire house.

The bridal party may depart for the hairdresser at staggered times, which means breakfast will become a movable feast that can go on right up until the wedding party leaves for the ceremony. Various relatives will arrive to have a sneak peek at the wedding party and they may expect to eat as well. Be prepared to iron, remove sudden stains, and have a needle and thread at the ready to repair any clothing mishaps.

One bride, who was a great admirer of Martha Stewart, ordered bouquets that were to be exact replicas of bouquets she'd spotted in a magazine. When the flowers arrived, they were indeed magnificent, but huge. Full-sized hydrangeas battled for attention with multiple long-stemmed roses. The arrangements were so heavy, the attendants couldn't hold them upright for any length of time. It was decided that the bridesmaids should lay the flowers across their left arm while steadying the entire array with their right arm. Unfortunately, the florist had not thought to remove the thorns from the roses. The florist shop was located a good forty-five minutes away from us. It was up to me to use our sharpest paring knife to remove every thorn from every rose. It was quite obvious that I was dealing with bouquets that cost upwards of four hundred dollars per arrangement.

I had to accomplish this task without losing a single petal or rearranging a single bloom.

At first we weren't prepared for the incredible mess the bridal party would leave behind upon their departure. We needed to deal with large amounts of tissue paper, price tags, discarded costume jewellery, underwear (both new and used), shoes, hair products, and oversized florist's boxes. All and sundry were scattered from one end of the establishment to the other. The bridal party attendants generally don't expect to return to your place to spend the wedding night, but they will expect to collect their luggage and belongings at various times. Some will arrive at the door very late, after the wedding reception has ended. Others will turn up at various times during the next day. This means that you could lose one night's accommodation income on most or all of your rooms. A popular start time for wedding ceremonies is 2:00 p.m. Our check-in time at the B&B was 2:00 p.m. This made it impossible to get the place clean and restaged for a new set of guests. As weddings often happen during the peak tourism season, this can seriously affect your "bottom line."

A boutique inn located south of us that specializes in weddings demands a minimum two nights' booking for all weddings. They also demand that a wedding party book every room at the inn. To an outsider of the business, this may sound unreasonable. To those in the business, this is a very reasonable request.

Some bridal couples will realize that you have gone above and beyond for them, and they'll come back to spend their wedding night with you. We appreciated this and would make sure that a frosty split of champagne plus fresh flowers awaited them upon their return to their room. Offering a very flexible breakfast time the next day was always appreciated by the very tired couple.

Also on the upside, some couples returned for each following wedding anniversary. One very romantic husband always arranged to have roses in the most gorgeous shade of pale mauve delivered for his wife prior to their arrival.

We once had a professional wedding planner stay with us as she worked on a wedding taking place at a nearby venue. She had a TV show on a reality channel and both she and her husband were an absolute delight. On the day of the wedding, they went out early to collect wild lilacs to decorate the venue. Some of her past wedding-planning adventure stories had us in stitches. She told us about one bride whose gown was so wide she had to walk sideways down the church aisle. Her poor father attempted to walk with her but was completely invisible, as he was lost in the voluminous skirts of her dress. I sincerely hope this wedding planner writes a book about these experiences.

Over our fourteen years in the business, we had seventeen weddings launched out of our home, and had hundreds of wedding guests stay with us while they attended weddings in the area. We kept extra dress ties for those men who had forgotten that they should probably wear a tie with the suit they planned to wear that day. On one occasion, my husband loaned out a pair of dress shoes to a guest whose well-worn running shoes didn't pass inspection. We had a father of the groom, resplendent in his kilt, practising the bagpipes as he strolled up and down our front lawn. His special assignment was to pipe in the bride as she entered the church.

We once had to come to the rescue of a couple of wedding guests who were running late because they hit a deer as they sped to the ceremony. Another time, two couples staying with us were attending the same wedding in the small village of Walter's Falls. This tiny settlement has roads that radiate out in several different directions, some following the twists and turns of Walter's Creek as it flows through the village. Getting lost in Walter's Falls is a common occurrence and the General Store sells bumper stickers that proclaim "I got lost in Walter's Falls." The regional joke is "Don't ever stop and ask a local how to get out of the village. If they knew, they would have left years ago." Our two sets of wedding guests finally caught up with each other the next day at breakfast. They broke into gales of laughter when they met up in our dining room. One couple had managed to find the village church and witness the ceremony but could not find the community centre where the reception was being held. The other couple missed the ceremony but did manage to find the reception. Twice, the couples had passed each other in their quests, one car driving one way and the other driving in a completely different direction.

Shortly before selling the house, we were honoured to offer the space to a young bride who had worked for us for several summers while she was in high school. The wedding ceremony was to be held at the family farm. At this point in time, we had closed down our business, so we happily turned over the entire house to her. We arrived in time to see the wedding party in all their finery.

The bride was extremely nervous but only because her dad had refused to tell her what vehicles he would be using to transport the wedding entourage from our place to the farm. She was expecting a flotilla of tractors and wagons to come down our driveway. She was extremely happy when a procession of vintage, highly collectible automobiles rolled up to our front door to whisk away a much relieved bride and all of her supporters in great style.

Deciding to sell our home was a very difficult and emotional decision for us. Seeing this lovely bride of whom we are so fond departing to start her new life began to complete the circle for us. We knew the house had almost done all it was supposed to do while we were its owners. Our separation anxiety began to ease a little. We had owned the house for twenty-four years and had run the Bed and Breakfast business in it for fifteen years. We were very attached to the house and to the business we had run there.

Chapter 12

Of Waifs and Wanderers

Apart from requested viewings of our rooms, we often got other unexpected knocks on our door, which brought us people looking for a "port in the storm." One rainy Sunday morning, the doorbell rang right in the middle of our breakfast service. Standing outside were two very wet and bedraggled young people, each holding a wet bedroll and a sopping backpack. They'd been camping on the Bruce Trail and were completely flooded out during the night. Their cellphone didn't survive. Feeling cold and miserable, they just wanted to call their parents to come and take them home. The young man's parents lived a good two-and-a-half-hour drive away, while the young woman's parents lived in the area. We fed them copious amounts of waffles and, after our other guests and the young man's hiking partner had departed, had the opportunity to hear his story.

He was a university student and had just completed a work semester in Fort McMurray. He'd earned a large amount of money and had enough put aside to pay for his next year of schooling and to pay off any outstanding debts. When he realized that he wouldn't need to work for the summer, he thought, *What have I always wanted to do?* He said that, as a boy, he'd always spent a great deal of time outdoors and had become very observant of the native flora and fauna surrounding him. It suddenly came to him that what he needed was to walk the entire Bruce Trail, from its start in Niagara Falls to its completion in Tobermory. He decided to travel lightly, camp along the way, and, as much as possible, forage for his meals using what nature presented to him as he followed his quest. He showed us a book he was carrying with him that outlined most of the edible plants and berries to be found in the "wilds" of our province.

I must admit I felt a little uncomfortable when he showed us the chapter on edible mushrooms. He went on to tell us that he'd spotted at least five types of edible greens along the side of our long country driveway. He then proceeded to run outside and soon returned with a weed that I'd grown to hate because it attacked our gardens in a most invasive manner. "I'll make you a tea from the seeds on this plant and you'll love it," he said. I must admit, it did taste better than we'd anticipated, but I still couldn't rid myself of my intense dislike for that particular piece of greenery, known as false chamomile or pineapple weed.

He went on to tell us that, as a young child, he'd always stopped to watch ants going about their daily business as well as watching myriad other birds and insects in their natural habitat. He explained that as he grew older, he had lost that capacity for keen observation but that after a month of hiking, it had all come back to him. He added that some days he travelled a very short distance along the trail because he'd spent a good deal of the daylight hours watching a bird build its nest or some other interesting phenomenon of nature at work.

After a few days at home with his parents, he planned to continue his trek and he expected to arrive in Tobermory by Labour Day. Our unexpected breakfast guest was all of twenty-two years of age, yet he shared with us a wealth of knowledge that showed a depth of wisdom well beyond his years. We didn't hear from him as to whether or not he completed his journey successfully. We didn't really ever expect to hear the outcome of this encounter, as the reality of running a B&B is that you get little snapshots of people's lives but, often, never an end to a particular story. This young man was an exception to that. He took one of our business cards with him when he departed that rainy Sunday morning.

Three years later, we received a phone call from him. "I've cleaned out my bedroom many times," he said, "but I never threw out your business card. I'd like to come and stay with you. And I'm bringing someone very special with me." He arrived with a lovely young lady. It was a new relationship, and they'd just returned from an autumn kayaking trip to some of the remote, uninhabited islands off the tip of Tobermory. He decided, after asking her to accompany him on such an arduous voyage, that he'd better treat her to a night or two in our Bed and Breakfast.

Before coming to us, they'd hiked through some of the wilder trails in Harrison Park in Owen Sound. Just off the trail, they'd discovered edible berries and mushrooms.

He proceeded to set up a cookstove in our side garden and prepare for his new love interest a delicious smelling evening meal. They stayed with us two more times after that, and these were always precious times filled with riveting stories about their latest adventures and a great deal of laughter. We hold dear our memories of the times spent with these two young people. Indeed, these two also rate their own book, not just a chapter in this one.

Chapter 13

Of Hikers and Bikers

Hikers, bikers, and motorcyclists make for wonderful guests at a B&B. Each group has a unique but reasonable set of needs based on the activity they are involved in. Hikers like an early and hearty breakfast containing lots of carbohydrates and protein. We set 7:00 a.m. as the earliest we'd provide a full-cooked breakfast, but some would have preferred 6:00 a.m., or even earlier. At first, we couldn't grasp why we were being asked to have breakfast so early, when the hikers often didn't depart until several hours later. Then we came to realize that they liked their breakfast to "settle" before they started off.

Our guests didn't realize that we rose two hours before the first breakfast to prepare the individual coffee and tea trays that we placed outside their doors. Preparing full packed lunches also took time. Sometimes not all of our guests were hikers, so we would find ourselves serving later breakfasts to other guests.

We did ask that all of our guests start their breakfast no later than 9:00 a.m. There were always a few who felt that this couldn't possibly apply to them. They would have their coffee on the side porch and then amble in to dine at 10:00 a.m. or later. This meant a real scramble to get dishes washed, dining room and kitchen clean, and bedrooms turned out and ready to receive new guests for 2:00 p.m. check-in. On several occasions we had new guests arrive as we were bidding other guests goodbye. The new arrivals were often hours early for check-in but wanted to drop off their belongings and view their room before heading out for their day. We had to politely tell them that they were welcome to stow their belongings in our private living room, but that they would have to wait to view their room. This also meant that we had to carry all of their things to their bedroom once the room was prepared. In the later years of running the Bed and Breakfast, we had teenage employees who were very capable of quietly working on the rooms that had been vacated while we dealt with the guests who were lingering. The whole process was exhausting, and we became very proficient at grabbing a power nap later in the day when time allowed for such a luxury.

  David provided a drop-off and, if necessary, a pick-up service at the various trailheads in the surrounding area. He became very familiar with each trailhead within a large catchment area. Some of the entry and exit points are very obscure and present a real challenge, even to the most experienced hiker. It would sometimes take over an hour to accomplish this service because the first stop would be where the hikers planned to end the day. They would leave a vehicle or their bicycles there so that they had transportation when they finished their trek. Then David would drive them to the spot they'd chosen to begin their hike. Some people would stay with us while they were hiking the Beaver Valley, which meant an hour drive each way.

We probably didn't charge as much as we should have for this service but instead viewed it as a unique perk we could offer our guests. We had to carry extra insurance on our vehicle in order to do this, and of course the fluctuating price of gas also affected our bottom line.

After several years of offering this service, word got around through the "hikers' grapevine," and a few people tried to take advantage of our willingness to do this. One group of ladies phoned and said, "We think your B&B is very cute. We don't want to stay with you, but we would like you to pick us up and drop us off at the trailheads in your area." Another gentleman phoned multiple times demanding that we get him from his location in the Beaver Valley and deliver him to his campsite at a local KOA. At one point, we had three groups of hikers all staying with us at the same time. Each asked to be dropped off at a different location at the exact same time. We learned to be very specific about the perks we offered.

Many of our guests would walk up to thirty kilometres a day. The sections of the Bruce Trail through our area are particularly steep, rough, and challenging. One of us always stayed at the house whenever we had guests on the trail, in case they ran into trouble and we needed to go and get them or to send help. This happened only twice, and each time the problem was fairly easily sorted. The recurring issue was hikers who didn't keep up with the rest of their hiking party. It's quite easy to get separated from the group. Experienced hiking groups always have a "sweeper" who brings up the rear and makes sure everyone is accounted for. Each section of the Bruce Trail has a dedicated volunteer who walks the trail often and makes sure there are no tree branches or anything across the trail and ensures the blazes (diamond-shaped signs) are legible and have not become overgrown as the season progresses.

We had one group of hikers who phoned partway through the day and said, "We're at trail marker 276. Where are we?" I was at a loss as to how to help them because the Bruce Trail is not marked numerically. The group had turned onto a winter skidoo trail instead of going straight ahead and remaining on the hiking path. They told us later that they should have known better because there should be a visible blaze every ten minutes or so. As the skidoo trail was wide and, as they admitted, they were deep in conversation, it took about half an hour before they realized that all wasn't as it should be. Needless to say, their hike added about an hour to their day, and they were exhausted when they finally got back to us.

For guests who just wanted a taste of hiking on the Bruce Trail, we often suggested side loop trails they could manage in under an hour.

Spring and fall are the prime times to hike because the weather tends to be cooler and there are fewer biting insects. Veteran hikers will hike regardless of the weather. If they hike in the rain, the wise B&B host will have shallow pans of water waiting outside the door to wash off muddy boots. Old newspapers will also be needed to stuff inside leather boots so they don't shrink as they dry. We always had tea and cookies ready for our guests upon their return, and our foot spa got quite a workout.

Sometimes guests arrived late in the day but were determined to try out the Bruce Trail immediately and refused to listen to our advice about how quickly darkness can fall in the forest. On two such occasions, I had my face pressed up against our front window, peering into complete darkness and wondering if we should call the OPP to begin searching. Luckily, in both cases, the hikers found their way back to the main road by listening for the noise of passing cars. Only one group admitted that they were really quite frightened by their experience. The trail often runs beside deep crevices.

It's extremely dangerous to stray off the trail. Cell phone reception has improved considerably, but there are still dead areas on the trail where there is no reception. Phoning for help is not always possible. Getting caught on the trail after dark is a recipe for disaster.

One early November day a few years ago, two got caught on the trail as night fell. They managed to call the OPP and two officers rushed onto the trail and became lost in the darkness. One of their cellphones had no reception while the other worked only at intervals. The volunteer fire department had to position themselves on the highest hill in the area in order to establish any sort of phone connection with the police. Eventually, two very embarrassed officers and two very worried hikers were all rescued, but it became a cautionary tale we often told skeptical novice hikers.

"Were the hikers staying with you?" they always asked.

"Thankfully, no," we would reply.

A local story circulated later that same fall about two elderly brothers who had told their wives that they were going to Meaford harbour to look at boats. Nightfall came and the men were nowhere to be found. Finally, their car was located at the trailhead of a particularly treacherous portion of the Sydenham Loop of the Bruce Trail. The police knew it was far too dangerous to enter the trail at that time of night. They prepared to enter the next morning, expecting to find the worst-case scenario due to the advanced age of the hikers. Just as they were about to enter the trailhead, out wandered the two elderly gentlemen. They were tired and thirsty but otherwise quite healthy. They'd realized that they had to stop walking the trail when it became dark. They were afraid that if they sat down, they'd be too cold and stiff to get up the next morning. Their solution was to stand and hug each other for warmth while singing songs and telling stories from their past. Their strategy worked.

One October, we had a group of repeat hikers stay with us. They knew we were expected to work at a large annual turkey BBQ at our local community centre and assured us that, since they were veteran hikers, we should go ahead instead of staying home in case they needed us. They definitely would not get into any trouble. Earlier in the day, they'd left their car at the trailhead where they expected to end their day. Their hike went perfectly, and their car was right where they left it. What they didn't have, however, were their car keys. They knew we would be up to our ears carving turkeys and helping to serve over two hundred dinners, so they opted to phone a local taxi company. Mind you, this was before the days of cellphones with GPS coordinates, and they were stranded on a very obscure part of the trail. "Don't worry," the cabby reassured them. "I'll find you." They weren't so confident and had just about given up hope when out of the dusk and the gloom rolled a quite ancient taxi with a rather rotund driver behind the wheel. Fortunately, a different hiker had been in charge of the house key, so it all ended well, and they were even able to enjoy takeout turkey dinners from the community centre event.

Bicyclists brought us a whole new range of experiences and stories to tell. We had a cyclist from Switzerland who arrived at our door early one afternoon. He hadn't made a reservation with us but explained that he'd underestimated the number of steep hills along the route and was exhausted. We did have a room available, and David suggested that we would be happy to wash his very smelly biking clothes while he slept. Of course, David was far more diplomatic than to say that the fellow reeked to high heavens, but they both knew what David was talking about.

We heard absolutely nothing from his room for twenty-four hours and became quite concerned about his "well-being." Also, as he hadn't paid for his room, we began to wonder if we were about to experience our first bed-and-dash client. We ended up sleeping on the couch in the living room, close to the front door, so that we could hear our mysterious guest if he decided to make a midnight departure. As we had single women staying in the other rooms in the house, we were also somewhat concerned for their safety. The next morning, our guest finally appeared around 9:00 a.m. He apologized profusely for sleeping so long, thanked us for doing his laundry, and ate a substantial breakfast. He was a very fit young man and his athletic physique was well displayed in the newly washed Lycra biking outfit. Some of the ladies were quite taken with this affable and interesting young man. Several of them made repeat visits with us and always inquired upon booking if there was any chance they might get to dine with another Lycra-clad "hottie" as a bonus to their B&B stay.

A very interesting couple from the Netherlands arrived with bikes that had been shrink-wrapped and shipped to Canada for their historic trek. They'd made an in-depth study of the Underground Railroad used by runaway slaves. They'd started their lengthy trip in the southern United States and were following the exact path that the slaves had taken. As Owen Sound marks the end of the Underground Railroad, we welcomed them at the end of their three-month-long journey. They were extremely knowledgeable about this particular aspect of Canadian history. Their stories were fascinating and very well told, even though English was a second language for them. We were pleased to direct them to a Black-history museum in Thornbury, Ontario, that they hadn't heard about. They returned to us each day, brimming with excitement and eager to tell us about their latest discoveries. These two were well into their seventies and a true example of the saying that "age is merely a state of mind."

Hosting folks who arrived on bicycle also meant being prepared to offer them dinner as they were often reluctant to be on the road later in the day when it meant biking back in the dark. We had one guest who did decide to bike to a historic mill just south of us for dinner. On the way there, he was forced into the ditch by a speeding car and returned to us hungry and somewhat battered and bruised. It was then that we decided we needed to offer cyclists an evening meal.

Another day, I took a phone call from a very pleasant-sounding gentleman who inquired if we accepted motorcyclists. When I replied that yes indeed we did, he said, "Oh good, every once in a while the boys have gotta ride."

He went on to explain that "the boys" were all retired professional football players. "We like to eat," he said. "What do you serve for breakfast?" I began to list off some of the items that we might offer over a week at the B&B. "Good," he said. "That's what we'll have. We'll pay extra, of course." Needless to say, a trip to the supermarket was needed before these guests arrived. Later in the day, five fully decked-out Harley Davidson motorcycles came thundering down the drive. My husband was beside himself with joy. He was also a little worried. "Do you realize how much money is sitting in our parking lot? I'm going to have to sit up all night to make sure no harm comes to any of those high-end machines."

The "boys" were all family men of a certain age. They were funny and very easy to have in the house. And they could eat! There were no leftovers after that particular breakfast.

Chapter 14

Hunters, Gatherers, and Hikers Too

Over our many years in the business, we hosted a number of nature lovers. These people taught us to truly appreciate the Niagara Escarpment biosphere that surrounded us and the Bruce Trail that wound past our home. Some would return from their outings with hundreds of beautiful photos that they were anxious to share.

One of our nature-loving hikers who was assigned the task of sweeper was an avid photographer. Her job was to walk at the end of a long line of hikers to make sure that the group stayed together and everyone arrived safely at the appropriate trailhead at the end of the hike. She returned each day with detailed photos of mosses, lichens, uniquely shaped leaves, and wind-sculpted trees. Any number of these photos were worthy of showcasing in an art gallery. She told us that the group always had to wait for her at the completion of each day of hiking. She often kept them waiting for up to an hour. However, over a glass of wine and appropriate snacks back at our B&B, they were just as excited about her photographic discoveries as she was. One gentleman admitted that, before joining this group of hikers, he had prided himself on setting speed records for the completion of various sections of the trail each day and he'd had no idea how much he was missing as he sped along the trails. There may not have been any roses to stop and smell, but the entire group had become much more aware of the wonders of the environment as they completed each leg of their journey.

Sometimes guests returned to the house with wild leeks, wild ginger, and watercress that we happily incorporated into their morning meal. Other hikers were delighted to tell David which streams were providing a home for various game fish.

When we first opened our Bed and Breakfast, the Bruce Trail ran far south of us, and catering to hikers wasn't part of our initial business plan. We'd been open about a year when the Sydenham Bruce Trail Club decided to embark on the longest trail reroute the association had ever undertaken. The project added 120 kilometres to the Bruce Trail and attracted a lot of hikers to the immediate area. We had to quickly educate ourselves about the very specialized needs of this new client base.

We were privileged to host some unique hikers. A woman and her eighty-year-old mother spent time with us while they hiked the trail. The mother had hiked the El Camino trail in Spain as well as trails in British Columbia and South America. Hiking the Bruce Trail was on her bucket list. Various family members were each taking a week's holiday so that they could hike with her. Her daughter, who was not yet retired, had asked if her mom could wait to do this. She said her mom gave her a look and replied, "I'm eighty years old. No, I can't wait to do this hike." They walked and talked, sang, and shared memories as they did their daily trek. They were in bed and fast asleep by 8:00 p.m. each night but up at the crack of dawn every day. What wonderful memories they were storing up for the entire family.

Another young couple was raising money for research into a rare disease that his mother was suffering from. His girlfriend was a musician, and he was the hiker. They had an online following, and she gave concerts in various towns along the trail. They called their project He Walks, She Rocks. As our contribution to their very worthwhile venture, we didn't charge them for their stay.

We had hikers who were determined to walk the entire trail from start to finish in one month. We had a long-distance runner who attempted to run the entire trail. This was a dangerous undertaking because our portion of the trail involves routes into crevices and over rock falls as well as the ever-present danger of tree roots. However, he managed to carry this out with nary a bruise. We hosted a retired structural engineer who had volunteered to inspect every fence stile and foot bridge along the trail. This often required him to crawl underneath structures, and he would return at the end of the day covered with the red pigment from the clay.

After experiencing guests wandering around in our kitchen as we tried to prepare breakfast, we decided to deliver coffee and or tea trays outside each guest's bedroom door, a half hour before their prearranged breakfast time. This could be quite a challenge. We offered a selection of over forty different herbal teas. Sometimes I found myself preparing four different trays to be delivered at four different times. I would set the trays out on our kitchen table the night before. Each tray had a Post-it note outlining important details, such as type of coffee (caffeinated, decaffeinated, dark roast, medium, mild) whether they wanted milk or cream or both, and even an exotic tea request here and there (chai tea with frothed milk on top). It was a bit like landing airplanes, I suppose. Trying to get the correct trays to the correct doors at the correct time was quite a challenge and necessitated my having a large and strong cup of coffee myself before attempting the feat.

David would wait for some of this early morning dust to settle and then would do some of the cooked entrées while I waited on the tables. Unless requested to do so, we never served plain bacon and eggs. We always tried to serve something that people probably wouldn't take the time to prepare for themselves at home. The menu was posted the night before, and we had a Plan B, just in case there was an issue with our selected offering. When people made their bookings with us, we always inquired as to any special dietary needs.

One family of five who stayed with us for several nights each had their own special requirements. One member was lactose intolerant, two had gluten issues, another could not eat eggs, and one was a vegan. We had other guests there at the time who, upon viewing this challenge, stated to us privately that they would be happy to eat whatever was placed in front of them.

Ironically, when the family of five checked out and we cleaned out the room of the teenage son, we found evidence of drug use plus a baggie of a dubious substance tucked up into the bed springs. We also found one of the spoons from our breakfast table hidden in his room, the bowl of which contained the remains of a melted substance. So much for being so concerned about what food he was putting into his body.

As previously mentioned, David was the night owl, so he always stayed up to greet late arrivals. Some Bed and Breakfasts have very strict rules as to check-in times. If one wishes for their business to be successful in a high tourist area, this particular house rule does not work if you wish to keep your rooms full. The last ferry boat from Manitoulin Island to Tobermory arrived at 10:00 p.m. People would frequently disembark and then drive to the Owen Sound/Meaford area, and this meant they would be well located for their next day of sightseeing. An arrival time of midnight or even later wasn't unusual. It also meant these folks had to be delivered to their room as quietly as possible so as to not awaken other guests. This was very challenging if the new guests arrived bearing takeout food. They expected that you would provide plates and silverware and cope with the smell of french fries and other fast foods wafting throughout the entire house. Other guests would tell us the next morning that they experienced the strangest dreams during the night. "I thought I was in a fast-food restaurant, and I never eat fast food."

Another business partnership we formed involved a midnight shuttle service from a local wedding reception venue back to our home. The business hosting the reception was always relieved to know that their wedding guests, who may have been "over-served" while celebrating the nuptials, would not be attempting to navigate heavily wooded country roads inhabited by deer and other creatures. This service brought us an abundance of guests.

    I always got up a good hour and a half before David to prepare for breakfast. I took off my apron when waiting tables while David put an apron on for his part of the meal preparation. Guests would see him bedecked in some fancy chef's apparel and say, "Oh, David, you do all the cooking as well?" The first few times this happened he didn't rush to correct them. It took a strong stance and a small insurrection on the part of the "sous-chef" before he began to quickly clear up any misunderstandings about the division of labour in the kitchen. Working in a business with your life partner is a delicate dance. There were missteps and, at first, we weren't always in tune. Eventually, we reached a balance of rhythm and tempo that worked. We knew we'd reached that point when more than one guest remarked, "What a great way to make a living. You make it all look so easy."

Chapter 15

Yes, We Take Children

For obvious reasons, many B&Bs won't accept children under a certain age as guests. Many people choose to stay at a B&B with the expectation of finding a calm, quiet, and restorative atmosphere. And children are sometimes not a good match for these adult expectations.

The physical setup of our home allowed us to accommodate families in the 1878 portion of the house and then close the door between that older section of the house and the newer addition. The thick stone walls of the farmhouse contained any excess merriment, and we had the option of feeding the family at our large pine kitchen table rather than in the more formal setting of the dining room. Most parents who choose to stay in a B&B know that their children will behave, so we had very few issues with our younger guests.

We once had one poor wee soul who was having a very difficult time with teething. However, only our two cats seemed bothered by this. The infant's wails must have hit a particular frequency that only animals could hear, as both cats sat at the bottom of the stairs with their hair standing on end. No one else in the house seemed to be aware that anything was amiss.

Our tabby cat, Barney, was particularly good with children. He would stretch out in front of them and let the kids pet him, however rough those caresses might be. He was at his happiest if there were two children, one to work on his front and one to stroke his back.

One summer we had a family of four from France spend several days with us. The mother was a travel agent in Paris; the father, a professor at a Parisian university. The little girls were four and five, and they spoke no English. When they arrived, the girls immediately began talking to us very energetically and all in French. Recalling my high school French lessons, I said, "Je parle seulement un peu français." (I speak only a little French.) They drew back and looked at me with great pity and then said "Un peu?" For the rest of their stay, they spoke to me very slowly and in a manner someone might adopt to address a person none too bright. Barney the cat made a much better impression. Each day, after arriving back at the B&B from their day's outing, they would hit the front entrance demanding, "Où est BARNEEE?" They would then climb to the top of the stairs, stand outside their bedroom door, and call "Barneee! Oh, Barneee!" Barney would trot past, giving us a very self-satisfied smirk, as if to say, *I've got this. See you later.*

On the last morning of their stay, both little girls were very tearful. We realized that they were extremely sad to leave Barney. We gave them a photo of him peeking through our garden gate and made them understand that the photo was theirs to keep. The littlest girl clasped the photo to her heart and said "Ah, le souvenir de Barnee." For days after their departure, Barney would, quite literally, stomp past, stop, turn, and look back at us, as if to say, *Okay, what did you do to make those two cute little kids leave?*

When you're running a B&B, keeping pets can be problematic. We made quite sure that our two felines neither entered a guest's room nor begged for food at the table. Repeat guests often arrived with treats and toys for the cats, and on a number of occasions, both Barney and Decker received presents in the mail from various past guests.

Barney was quite the little actor. When the professional photographer arrived to take photos for our website, Barney followed him from room to room and then proceeded to pose in the most flattering way possible. Finally, the photographer gave in and took a few snaps of the furry boy. We decided to use one of these photos on our website as a heads-up for prospective guests that there were two cats in residence.

Surprisingly, we lost very few reservations due to our furry family members.

Chapter 16

Affairs of the Heart

As guests came and went through our busy Bed and Breakfast, we were gifted with small snapshots of their equally busy lives. People sometimes left just as quickly as they arrived because they wanted to see and do as much as possible while visiting the area.

We often wished that we could, somehow, be privy to the next chapter in their lives. On rare occasions, we were given that chance.

Two years into our business venture, we began to get a series of emails from someone whose email address included the name "the Caped Crusader." The crusader's requests were very specific. The person was interested in booking our Fireplace Room. They wanted to know what views could be seen out of every window. As this was a large corner room, there were three different vistas to describe. The person also wanted to know if the fireplace could be viewed from the bed. Then they wanted to know if we provided vegetarian breakfasts, and could we please send a detailed menu for each of the three mornings they would be staying with us?

We didn't know whether to be relieved or very worried when the Caped Crusader finally made a confirmed booking with us. We could not have been more surprised when the loveliest young couple arrived at our front door. He was Canadian and she lived in England. They'd met while backpacking in New Zealand. This was her first trip to Canada; she'd just met his family, and now he wanted to show her a bit of Ontario. And he wanted her experience to be perfect, hence all the attention to detail in his emails.

They were very sweet together and very obviously in love. Our sense of humour matched their sense of fun, and they were as interested in the stories we had to tell as we were fascinated to hear about their adventures.

She was a keen bicyclist, and their new relationship even withstood a very lengthy, hot, and difficult bike ride along a coastal route that ran from Owen Sound to Wiarton. She was thrilled with that particular adventure, though he wasn't.

After they left, I said to David, "If ever two people were meant to be together, it's those two. I'm so sad we'll never know the end of their story." That Christmas we got a phone call from the Caped Crusader. "She's coming back to Canada for Christmas," he told us. "Can we come to you for a few days?"

They arrived at our front door, both sporting huge grins. "We're engaged!" they said. There were lots of details to work out regarding work visas and the melding of two sets of parents, both from entirely different backgrounds, but they worked through it all. These two lovely people now have three charming children. They continued to book holidays with us. It was amusing to watch as the sports car and minimal luggage morphed into a family-sized vehicle as each new child joined the family. We were delighted to be asked to be honorary grandparents to their firstborn and had both sets of grandparents stay with us on several different occasions. We do enjoy a good love story with a happy ending.

This same couple recommended us to a long-time friend who booked with us one March break. His girlfriend was in her first year of teaching, and when they arrived, she wasn't feeling at all well. I sympathized with her and explained that, during my teaching career, getting sick during what was supposed to be a holiday was a very common event.

The couple asked us if there was some place where they could go hiking. There was still a lot of snow on most of the trails. We gave them a booklet of winter waterfall tours in the area and suggested that these might be more accessible. We didn't realize that they also picked up summer tourist information that we had on hand. They returned late in the afternoon and told us about their adventure. They had decided to hike into Bruce's Caves. We were astounded. This hike is challenging in good weather and not for the faint of heart in the winter. They explained that the sky was blue and birds were singing as they followed freshly made tracks through the snow. Suddenly they stopped to take a good look at those tracks. They could see what appeared to be claw marks at the front of each snowy imprint. Beside the tracks, there was another indentation that looked as if something was being dragged through the snow. "What would make those tracks?" they asked us.

"Bear," we replied.

"What was it dragging?" they asked.

"Lunch," we replied.

Later that evening, they headed out for dinner at a very funky diner located near the Meaford military base. Their friends had recommended the place because it has excellent food and is unique and very quirky. The next morning, they appeared at breakfast with huge smiles on their faces. "We're engaged!" they said.

"I feel much better, I'm not sick anymore," she said.

It was then that he told us the story of his attempt to find the perfect place in which to propose. He'd had the ring in his pocket as they made their dangerous hike to Bruce's Caves. "I'm from the city and I don't know much about reading tracks, but something told me that particular hiking trail wasn't a good place to get down on one knee." He went on to Plan B, which was to propose over a romantic dinner. No one had told him what a lively place the diner was or that all sorts of single guys with military haircuts would be there consuming large amounts of beer. "I decided to keep the ring in my pocket," he said.

"Good idea," we replied. "Probably half the diners there would have told your fiancée to accept the proposal, while the other half would have been hitting on her."

He finally resorted to Plan C, which was to propose in front of the fireplace at the B&B.

Fortunately we had learned to always keep champagne in the fridge as there were often such unexpected events that needed to be celebrated in-house.

Another couple, who often stayed with us, wrote their wedding vows while perched on an escarpment cliff overlooking the Beaver Valley. We became very close friends with them. When we sold our B&B and downsized, they took many of our much-loved family antiques to furnish a large Victorian home they were refurbishing. We were sad to let go of so many of these pieces of furniture, but it was comforting to know that they were going to a wonderful couple who would treasure each piece as much as we had. They even assured us that we had "visiting rights" and could see our former holdings whenever we wished.

We still correspond with the new owner of our old farmhouse, and she sends us photos of the gardens and lets us know when the various species of birds have returned in the spring. Her stories have become part of the evolving history of the house that hugs you.

Chapter 17

Turn Left at the End of the Driveway

The unique geographical location of our home meant we were often in a position that required us to hand out local maps and give detailed directions to lost travellers. My husband claims that I am the founder and past president of the See Ontario Unintentionally Club. If there is a way to get lost, I'll find it. I found it very easy to empathize with the confused travellers who arrived at our front door. Before the days of the GPS, I myself participated in some very interesting club rallies.

One club event included almost driving onto the end of a runway at Toronto Pearson International Airport. This was years ago, and I'm sure such an entrance no longer exists, but that escapade involved some fast talking with an RCMP officer who was stationed in a guard shack at the end of the runway. He just kept shaking his head with disbelief as I explained how this confused state of orienteering had come about. A friend who was travelling with me has never let me forget that particular adventure.

When the GPS was first introduced, it left much to be desired. The earliest mapping devices refused to recognize fire numbers, which, for country dwellers, is a municipal address. We frequently had confused guests phone us as they were sitting in front of the Owen Sound post office, a good twenty-five minutes away. They had plugged our rural route number and postal code into their GPS and it directed them to the source of that address, which was the city post office.

Another time, a group of determined hikers who wished to check in with us before embarking on the trail kept phoning and demanding our street address. They couldn't believe that a six-digit number was our address. They became more and more irritated with us. Finally, my husband gave them the address of our community centre, which is located in the hamlet of Woodford. It does actually have a street number. The group of five experienced hikers drove right past our driveway, and the large sign for our business located there, and proceeded to call us from the front of the community centre. "We are here, where are you?" they asked. We were somewhat concerned about the orienteering skills they would need in order to navigate the trails of the Niagara Escarpment. Somehow they managed to make it back to us at the end of each day of hiking.

Over the years, we experienced various lost souls in varying states of upset over their dilemma. A flustered and upset young lady who was maid of honour at a wedding needed immediate help, confused delivery people, and a couple who said they had made the trip to their cottage hundreds of times and had no idea how they could have gone so wrong are all valid members of my club. They often required a calming cup of tea as well as directions.

A big part of hosting guests from outside the area is the need to possess detailed knowledge of the local area. Upon their arrival, we would ask guests what they were hoping to see and do during their visit. We had maps and tourist information brochures, as well as pre-printed half-day and full-day trip suggestions that would lead the travellers in a logical circular route that would eventually bring them back to our B&B. This seemed to work well for people, and we got very positive feedback from guests who had decided to follow our recommendations.

We once had a mother, father, and three children from the western United States check in with us for a lengthy stay. If the "Unintentionally Club" had been having a membership drive, this family would have met the qualifications to attain premier membership status. Each day they would ask for suggestions for places to go and things to see. They wanted to explore the entire Bruce Peninsula as well as sites closer to the B&B. Each day we gave them detailed directions, starting with "Go to the end of the driveway and turn left." They would pore over the directions as they ate breakfast, then they would convene in the guest living room and again study the directions, speaking to each other in hushed tones. Finally, the group would make their way out to the family car. They would sit in the car for at least ten minutes, again discussing things with heads bent over our directions. Finally, the car would start up. They would drive to the end of the driveway and ... turn RIGHT. *Well, there's the start of another disastrous day*, we would think.

Hours later they would return. "Did you have a nice day?" we would ask.

"Not really," they would reply. "We couldn't find one thing on your suggestion list. We did have dinner at one of your more popular restaurant chains though."

"Oh, where did you eat?" we inquired.

"Some place called Tim Hortons," they replied. "They certainly don't have a very extensive dinner menu, do they?"

When we asked the children what they would remember about their vacation in Ontario, they replied, "Making U-turns. That's all we ever did." Upon leaving us they wanted to visit an island. The most obvious choice would have been to travel to Manitoulin Island, but they decided the ferry ride was too expensive and instead they would go to Christian Island. We tried to explain to them that that particular island was relatively small and home to mostly private summer homes. There would not be many tourist areas to visit there. They looked at us skeptically and announced that the family had decided that this was their next stop. Long after their departure, we had visions of their family sedan circling the wilds of Northern Ontario, stopping for numerous family conferences on the side of the road, after which the driver would make a U-turn.

Chapter 18

Don't Ever Do That, Mate

Our list of B&B owner dos and don'ts continued to grow as time went by.

We were in England the first time we enjoyed a morning tea tray left outside our bedroom door. However, we decided that we would never utter the very English term that we heard during our time in Devon. The host said, "Our son will bring you a tea tray and knock you up in the morning." In England this simply means that someone will gently knock on your bedroom door when they deliver the tea tray. In Canada this expression has a totally different and very rude meaning. We must have looked very shocked the first time we had this message delivered to us.

One Ontario Bed and Breakfast, where we stayed for three nights, thrust a hospital-like menu card into our hands the very minute we stepped inside their front door. A card for each day of our stay was to be filled out by putting a check mark in a small box beside each breakfast item. We discovered the hard way that very dry toast would not be accompanied by anything else unless you placed the appropriate check mark beside butter, jam, or peanut butter. We also quickly learned that we were going to be drinking our coffee black unless we checked off the box for cream and another spot for sugar. An elderly aunt, who was very hard of hearing, delivered our pre-ordered items and quite literally turned a "deaf ear" when we tried to amend our incorrectly ordered breakfast. The menu itself was very limited. The entrées available included bacon and eggs **OR** pancakes **OR** dry cereal. (Don't forget to order some milk.) The use of an extra dark font for each of the **ORs** spoke volumes as to the rigidity of the menu selections. It certainly didn't make allowances for a guest with a large appetite. Nowhere on the menu card did it say **All of the Above**.

One morning we breakfasted at the same time as a young couple who were spending their weeklong honeymoon at this establishment. They didn't hesitate to tell us that they were finding the sparse breakfast selection to be very tedious. They ordered the same breakfast day after day and were very much looking forward to the end of their stay. This situation was carefully entered on the DON'T side of our B&B list.

This same business placed a rule book in each guest room. This book was so large and so detailed it took two hands to heft it. It could have supplied us with several hours of bedtime reading. After perusing the first two pages of military type commands, we hid the book away and didn't refer to it again. In their advertising, this B&B had extolled the delights of their outdoor hot tub. Pages two and three of the detailed handbook were devoted to all the rules concerning the use of this feature. There was an extensive list of requirements, which included booking your twenty-minute time of usage within very limited hours of availability. We decided to take a pass on that particular experience. During our three-day stay, we didn't witness anyone using that hot tub. We decided that this was a very effective way to cut down on the cleaning and maintenance of such an amenity.

During our years of running a B&B, various guests delighted in regaling us with their own tales of stays in other B&B establishments.

The majority of guests would tell us that they liked hosts who were there for them if they needed them but who didn't "hover" when the guests were seeking some "alone time." This is a difficult balance. Often, guests would arrive on a Friday evening with their shoulders drawn up tightly with stress and they would speak to us in very curt tones. The first few times this happened, we worried that the stay wasn't going to go well. However, after a good night's sleep and time out in the peace and quiet of the country setting, these same people would chat away to us like long lost friends and there would be hugs all around when it was time for them to leave.

Most guests don't like a situation where they never see the host or indeed even a hint that the host is somewhere in the house and on call if there should be an emergency. A friend told us about a rather unnerving experience at a B&B in a summer theatre town. She arrived at the establishment with three other female friends to find that, although they had arrived at the prearranged time, no one answered their repeated knocks at the door or the ringing of the doorbell. They were pressed for time as they had a dinner reservation that preceded the evening performance at the local theatre. Finally, one of the theatre goers tried the door. It was open. They entered an empty and eerily silent house.

On the kitchen table was a very terse note. It contained the name of each guest and a number after it, which they assumed must be their room number. They crept through the entire house, locating the properly numbered doors as they went. They changed for their evening out and decided that perhaps the business owner had another job and would be there to meet them when they returned from dinner and the show.

After a wonderful theatre production, the ladies were relieved to see lights on in the home as they returned that evening. They again entered a totally silent and very empty feeling home. There was a new and, again, very terse note waiting for them. The note asked them to please use the pen provided to indicate their desired breakfast time and if they preferred coffee or tea in the morning. That night, they each pushed a chair up under the door handle of their bedroom door, as they were feeling distinctly uncomfortable about trying to sleep in what appeared to be an otherwise empty house. They reassured themselves that they would likely encounter their mystery host and/or hostess at breakfast the next morning.

They awakened to the smell of fresh coffee and felt that this was a positive sign. Upon entering the dining room, they found coffee in a thermal carafe, fresh fruit, and several hot entrées waiting for them on heated trays. Breakfast was totally self-serve, very delicious, but ominously available without the benefit of a greeter or a chef. Another note awaited them. It told them how much each guest owed for their night's accommodation and stated unapologetically that the establishment accepted cash only. This necessitated a quick dash to an ATM. Each woman left the appropriate cash with a note attached. One note said THANK, the second note said YOU, the third VERY, and the fourth note said MUCH.

Do not ever do this to your guests, the storyteller warned us. She said that they began to look for nanny cams, peep holes in the eyes of portraits hanging on the wall, and one even suggested that they rap on walls looking for a secret tunnel. She said that from then on, they would always refer to that B&B as "The House of the Phantom Host." It wasn't a spot they would ever recommend to friends.

An Australian work mate told us another cautionary tale about a B&B experience he and his partner had in Newfoundland. They were greeted at the door by a pleasant woman who showed them to a room that was obviously a family member's own private bedroom. The closet was stuffed full of clothing, as were all the dresser drawers. This friend is fairly easygoing and he said that this wasn't really a big problem for them, as they were just staying for one night.

A breakfast time was agreed upon for the next day, which happened to be a Sunday morning. Being very punctual, our friend and his companion arrived in the dining room to be met by the good lady of the house. She was dressed in her Sunday best, with a hat on her carefully coiffed hair and a purse over her arm. "Eat up," she said. "I leave for mass in ten minutes."

He said that they shovelled down their meal, trying very hard not to laugh too loudly at the absurdity of the situation. "We would have been happy to eat at an earlier time," he said. Then, fixing us with a very stern eye, he said, "Don't EVER do that, mate."

We took the advice to heart.

Chapter 19

Afraid? Not Really

We have often been asked if we found it frightening having "strangers" stay in our home. We had very few occasions when our "spidey" senses told us we might need to be wary. I always credited this more highly developed sense of impeding trouble to my many years of teaching. Going with one's "gut feeling" usually proves to be the right decision.

During our many years in the B&B business, we had an assortment of lost and thirsty hikers, plus exhausted, dehydrated joggers turn up at our front door and ask for assistance. If at all in doubt, we would invite these various folks to sit in the shade provided by our side porch. We would bring them water and juice and, if they appeared hungry, an assortment of baked goods left from that morning's breakfast. They would depart as they felt able and we had no negative events with any of these people.

Only once did we have people steal from us and that was an unexpected and disappointing occurrence. We had a family phone us from a distance away. They lived in the Canadian west but were on their way to Tobermory, where they intended to take the ferry to Manitoulin Island. There were two preteen girls, a mother and a father, and a new puppy, which they were picking up from a breeder in Ontario. They assured us that the puppy would remain in a kennel on the porch and, as our other guests would be housed in an entirely separate part of the house, we hoped that we could make this overnight stay work successfully.

We were somewhat surprised when only the dad arrived with the two young daughters and the puppy in tow. He explained that he had left his wife in the emergency department at the Owen Sound hospital, as she was very unwell. He asked if we could look after both kids and the dog while he went back to the hospital to be with her. We would have been pretty cold-hearted to say no to this request.

The day stretched into early evening, so we fed the girls and helped them tend to the puppy, which was surprisingly quiet and well behaved. Around 9:00 p.m., we got a phone call from the dad, asking us if we could please put the girls to bed. We began to wonder if we had just been left with not one but two abandoned children, plus a very sweet but unexpected new pet. Our two cats weren't amused. Much to our relief, the mom and dad returned to the house around 2:00 a.m. and asked David if they could have a very early breakfast, as they wanted to catch the 8:00 a.m. ferry out of Tobermory. We explained that they were still a good two-hour drive from the boat, but they insisted that this was just fine and could they please have breakfast at 6:00 a.m.

Four hours later, we were up and fixing breakfast. There were many things that the mom would not eat, which we assumed was because of her lengthy visit to the ER the night before. She explained that she had decided to put herself on a rigid diet before leaving on vacation. This diet restricted her calorie intake to no more than 1,000 calories a day. Her elimination system was rebelling, which was why she had gone to emergency to try to get things "moving" as it were. I had to bite my tongue to keep from suggesting that perhaps an extended motor trip far away from home wasn't the best time to embark on this regime but had to sternly remind myself that "the customer is always right."

Three times they said goodbye to us before rushing back into the house for various reasons. They took such a long time to depart, we knew there was no chance they would get on to the first sailing of the day.

When it was obvious that they had finally gone, I began to clear the breakfast table. It was then that I realized that two of our bright-yellow linen napkins were missing. *Why would anyone take two napkins?* I asked myself. It was then that I realized two of our Victorian knife rests, which we used on the table to complement our antique china, were also missing. We figured that someone had used the napkins to wrap up the glass knife rests before pocketing them. When we went to clean the bedrooms, I found that a collectible Anne of Green Gables paper doll cut-out book, given to us by a neighbour, was also missing. It had been sitting high on a display shelf, so the two suspects, the young girls, must have climbed up on something so that they could reach the book. This event didn't engender fear in any way, but rather a deep disappointment in the behaviour of people for whom we had gone the "extra mile."

We decided you have to put such situations aside and concentrate on all the wonderful and honest people who cross your threshold.

The only time that we became really alarmed was during the unfolding of a newsworthy story that would make a good movie script. At that time, David was the chairperson of the board that managed our local community centre. Early one morning, he received a phone call from a neighbour who served as a volunteer firefighter. He explained that immediate access to the centre was required and asked that David come and unlock the building. When David arrived at the centre, the parking lot was full of marked and unmarked police vehicles of every description. Once the door had been opened, officers in uniform and what appeared to be SWAT garb rushed into the building without any explanation.

David returned home, only to receive another call asking if he could please return to the centre and switch the landline so that it would ring in the centre and not at our home. As there was no permanent staff at this very small centre, calls requesting information about bookings and events were redirected to our home phone. When David re-entered the centre, numerous officers were bent over large topographical maps of the area and all the officers were heavily armed. David carried out the necessary actions to switch over the phone and beat a hasty retreat. Again no explanation was supplied.

Later that day, two of our female hiking guests told us that as they were departing the trail after a day of hiking, two armed men in camouflage outfits had passed them without speaking a word to them. "Is it hunting season?" they asked. We weren't really sure how to answer this question.

    A day later, we learned that the Toronto police had followed a murder suspect to our area. Knowing that he was being followed, the suspect had lost control of his car and crashed in a heavily wooded area. The amount of blood at the scene of the crash suggested that the suspect was quite badly hurt and would not be able to travel far on foot. Because of the deep crevices and fissures in the surrounding escarpment rock, it was assumed that the badly injured suspect had fallen down into one of these "bottomless pits" and was, by then, quite dead. We only heard the story several days after the police command post request.

    This news really concerned us. If the man had turned up at our door, we would have assumed he had been in some sort of road accident and let him into the house while we phoned for help. Someone in authority should have contacted the various Bed and Breakfasts in the area, as it is the nature of the business to help those in trouble.

    Almost two weeks later, the suspect was found hiding in a seasonal home that had been closed up for the winter. He had built a shelter for himself in the basement, fashioned out of unopened bales of insulation, and was subsisting on the store of tinned goods kept in the kitchen cupboards.

    If you stood on the roof of our two-storey home, you could see the roof of the home where the fugitive was hiding. That's how close he was to us.

That "event" gave us pause to reconsider our "open door policy."

We determined that one needs to maintain the "accommodate" in accommodation, but it must be done with care and caution.

Chapter 20

In Sickness and in Health

Every once in a while, if you're very lucky, a family will come to stay with you whose presence in your home is a gift forever etched upon your heart.

Gail was a high school teacher in Midland, which gave us an immediate "professional" connection. In her "spare time" she was studying to be a United Church minister. As my dad had been a United Church minister, our personal connections ran deep.

Gail would often organize extended "girls away from home breaks" at our B&B for her sister, her very engaging elderly mother, and Gail herself. These would happen several times a year. Soon, her brother began to book time away from his demanding job so that he could join the family. Their mother, June, had worked at a juvenile detention centre for a good deal of her life. She had been widowed at a very young age and her children were exceptionally close to her. June wouldn't have reached five feet tall, even on her tiptoes, but she was feisty, funny, and a force to be reckoned with.

Gail was absolutely meticulous in her own appearance. Every arrival, for every stay, required numerous trips from her car with various outfits. Each ensemble was carefully ironed and flawlessly accessorized. She changed outfits several times a day. As he helped carry in her extensive wardrobe, David would tease her and ask, "How long did you say you were staying?" as yet another garment bag was toted up the stairs and into her room.

Gail had the itinerary for each day planned just as carefully as her outfits. The plans always included a day at Sauble Beach, dinner at the Harrison Park restaurant, and a pilgrimage to historic Leith Church. Gail was an art teacher and totally fascinated with the works of the Group of Seven. She was an ardent fan of Tom Thomson, who is buried in the graveyard behind Leith Church, and Gail always spent time at his graveside. "I must visit Tom," she would say.

As well as visiting his burial site, Gail had taken numerous camping trips to Canoe Lake, where Tom met his end in a canoeing "misadventure." The details of his death remain a mystery to this day. Was it an accident or was he a murder victim?

"When I die," Gail would say, "I want to be buried in Leith Cemetery." We would nod our heads to show that we understood and then go on to discuss lighter topics.

The family visited us on a regular basis for five years. In that time they became an important extension of our own family. Late one summer, when I was trying to organize the local community centre turkey dinner in the middle of a particularly busy hiking season, Gail phoned to make a reservation. "You sound stressed," she said. "Tell me what's wrong." I certainly had not meant to transmit my angst, but we were having great difficulty finding enough volunteers to run such a large event. Reluctantly, I told her the problem.

Several days later, Gail phoned back. "Turkey problem solved," she said. She had rounded up six volunteers, whom she would drive from Midland to work at the event. She had also contacted her brother, John, who lived in Oakville, and he agreed to drive up to help out as well. She had a personal goal to do one "random act of kindness" every day. Not a day went by that she didn't fulfill this goal.

A year later, David took a phone call from Gail. She told him that she had just been diagnosed with terminal cancer and the doctor had told her to "get her affairs in order."

"We are coming to you for our last family visit," she said. "We are visiting you because you always make us laugh."

When David gave me this news, I went weak at the knees. "How can we make them laugh?" I asked. "I just want to sit here and cry."

The whole family arrived together, after having experienced a family counselling session meant to prepare them for what was ahead. They were quiet when they arrived, and Gail's elderly mother was struggling with her emotions. Somehow we did find things to laugh about. We also found quieter, gentler moments to spend together.

Gail decided to forgo traditional cancer treatments, opting for more alternative methods. She defied all the odds and survived for another eight years. The family continued to visit us, but we could see the obvious effort and the subsequent fatigue that Gail was stoically battling.

"You know what?" she said one day. "Do you know what I am going to do the minute I get to heaven? I am going to look up my hero Tom Thomson and I am going to find out what really happened that day on Canoe Lake."

Gail is indeed buried in Leith Cemetery. She designed her grave marker herself. It shows a woman in a canoe, paddling across a lake. In the background are tall pine trees drawn in true Tom Thomson style. On the shore ahead of the woman waits a much loved pet dog. The grave stone is of soft grey granite. The artwork is done in stark black outline. In the sky above the lake is one bright, intensely yellow star. Beneath the star are printed several lines from her favourite Neil Young song.

As the very last big event at our B&B, just before we sold the house, we hosted the reception following Gail's graveside service. Everyone attending had chosen their outfits and accessorized with great care. We all knew that Gail would be watching from above and no one wanted to let her down. At Gail's funeral, her brother, John, asked me if I had started to work on the long-promised B&B book. When I told him that I was working on it, he asked, "Are we in it?"

"Oh yes," I replied. "There will be an entire chapter about all of you."

"Please use our actual names," he said. "Gail would like that."

So ... Gail Forbes ... this chapter is for you. From our heart to yours.

Chapter 21

Midnight Manoeuvres

Living close to a military base brought us some very interesting experiences.

When we first bought our home, a kind couple down the road cautioned us about some of the unusual military activities that might take place. The wife told us about a time when they had decided to go for an evening walk along the sideroad. Other neighbours, spotting them ambling by, had invited them in for a beer, as it was a very warm evening. By the time they departed to make their way home, darkness had fallen. This is an area with no street lights. At times the darkness is utter and complete as it envelops you. They were only halfway back to their own home when the wife announced that, thanks to the beer she had consumed, she was in urgent need of a bathroom. Her husband suggested that since they were out in the country and it was very dark, she should avail herself of the deep ditch that ran beside the road. She said she was just gathering herself back together and preparing to scramble up and out of the ditch, when an entire platoon of soldiers appeared, making their way along the ditch. They were in night camouflage gear, faces darkened, and all wearing night-vision goggles, which would have allowed the entire troop to witness what should have been a "private" moment. As they squished their way past her, they all politely greeted her with, "Evening, Ma'am."

I assured the storytellers that I wasn't much of a beer drinker, but we would be very careful about taking midnight strolls off our own property.

A few months later, we began to have as regular weekend guests a man who worked on the military base and his young wife, who stayed with us over a span of several months. He was very circumspect as to his exact position at the military base, but we surmised that he was training Canadian Armed Forces SWAT teams. It wasn't at all unusual to see him quietly leave the house shortly after midnight and then return in time to have breakfast with his wife. We knew enough not to ask any questions about his nocturnal activities.

One Friday evening, just as all of our guests had checked in, the front doorbell rang. Looking out the front window, I spotted a Light Armoured Vehicle, known as a Cougar, parked right in front of the house. These vehicles are very large and, as far as I was concerned, it was a tank. The vehicle occupants very wisely sent the youngest and best-looking young man to the door. He flashed deep dimples at me and inquired if they could have permission to "hide" their vehicle in our parking lot. He explained that they were playing "war games" and had to keep the intersection closest to our place under surveillance.

I checked with the guests to make sure that they would not be offended. Instead, they were all delighted by this unexpected excitement. One couple could not contain their glee as they ran out to take photos to send to their two teenage sons, who had opted to stay home and play video war games rather than spend a weekend away with their parents. The commanding officer then brought each of his troops in to be introduced. Luckily, we had an abundance of muffins, which they all tucked in to before using our washroom facilities.

"May I ask you an additional favour?" asked the lead officer. "There is another vehicle just like ours that also needs to hide in your yard. May I radio them to join us?"

Well, if you have one tank, you might as well have two. We agreed. Moments later, another equally large tank backed down the drive and neatly manoeuvred into a parking place right beside our brand-new raised garden that we had just finished paying for. We held our breath as we watched this show of driving skills.

The second group from the newest arrival came in to meet us. I inquired as to who the driver of the tank might be, as I wanted to congratulate him on his expert handling of such a big piece of equipment. "How does the driver see in order to back up?" I asked. The driver explained that he couldn't see a thing as he reversed. One of his comrades in arms watched out of the open turret on top of the vehicle and radioed directions to the driver. I'm glad we didn't know that as we watched that particular spectacle unfold.

The leader explained that they would probably need to spend the entire night in our yard, if that was all right with us. We told him that this wasn't a problem and that we would leave the front door unlocked so that they could use the downstairs washroom if needed. He looked at us in surprise and asked, "You would leave your door unlocked?"

We laughed and replied, "Now, let's see, two army tanks, sixteen fully armed military types ... we'd love to see someone try to break in."

Several days later, David and I discussed whether or not we should add a photo of the two military vehicles to our website. David thought the caption should read: "Yes, we've stepped up security at Holly Cottage." Upon further reflection, we decided that some future guests might not share our sense of humour and so the pictures remain in our own personal memories only.

Chapter 22

A Little Advice

Over our many years of running a Bed and Breakfast, we were asked all kinds of questions, often by folks contemplating embarking on such a venture themselves.

The husband of one such couple told us he thought it would be a great idea to open a B&B so that his wife could "keep busy." His wife told us, rather shyly, that she wasn't really very sociable and she could not imagine having strangers stay in her home. We tried to explain as tactfully as we could that it took two of us working flat out to keep the place up and running, and that you did have to be quite easygoing if you were planning to welcome people into your place of residence.

We had others tell us that they knew it was probably a lot of work, but that they intended to have staff do all the work while they sat back and watched the money roll in. You might be able to do this if you charge an exorbitant amount for each night's stay. You'd probably find that the expectations of your guests will rise along with the rising cost of your rooms, so consider your pricing carefully.

There will be unexpected costs. The B&B owner must be prepared for waterproof mascara stains on their newest and very expensive towels. And there is no delicate way to explain that romantic trysts will leave residual stains on your high-thread-count sheets that not even the dry cleaners can remove.

Many of our guests assumed that we purchased our food products from a restaurant supply company at a reduced rate. They were quite surprised to learn that we would have to order substantially greater quantities of food than we would use in a week before we could deal with such a supplier. Our food was purchased via local farm gate programs and from the supermarket.

Many of our guests requested and expected that we would only use locally sourced food products. We totally support that movement, but the costs involved are higher than traditional supermarket prices. The cost of doing this must be factored into the room cost.

We had other people tell us that it must be wonderful to run a B&B business because you can close up and take extended vacations whenever you wish. The advent of online booking has certainly made this more possible, but you still stand to lose a chunk of your business and particularly potential new clients every time you go away.

Some B&B owners are lucky enough to have a reliable person to come in and run their business while they are away. This initiative is not without its drawbacks. We had guests tell us a story about a large Victorian home B&B they stayed at when the owners had gone out of town for a family wedding, leaving a relative to run the business.

As the guests were descending the grand staircase on their way to breakfast, they caught the flicker of flames reflected in a large mirror hanging on the wall by the stairs. "I don't remember the dining room having a fireplace," one said. It was then that they realized one of the dining-room walls was on fire. The substitute host had been called away by a guest just as he'd put bacon under the broiler. The resulting fire totalled the kitchen and most of the wall that separated the kitchen from the dining room. None of the guests were served breakfast that morning.

Upon hearing that story, we all speculated as to the reaction of the poor owners when they returned from their short sojourn away from the business. David and I filed that story under "More Cautionary Tales."

Other things may happen while you're away that a less experienced person would not be prepared to handle. This can lead to a bad review in an online review site. It only takes one negative review for your establishment to lose a star in its rating.

We have heard stories of rival businesses writing fake bad reviews so that their own business will rise to the top of the online reviews for their catchment area. One can also hire review writers who will leave a glowing review even though they have never stayed at your establishment. These reviews are written in a template type of prose. A discerning reader can soon spot these phony reviews, as they all sound very much the same.

We had a couple come to us one winter weekend just before a huge snowstorm hit. David had travelled out of town and could not get back to the B&B due to road closures. The people later remarked in their B&B review that they didn't know if there really was a "David" as they had not actually met him. I was flabbergasted, as they were quite aware of his situation. He had sent them directions for the best route to take to get to the winter wedding that they had come to the area to attend. They told me several times that they were so grateful to him for sending them those detailed directions, as one of the other wedding guests had become stranded on a snow-closed highway. I had assumed that they knew that what I was telling them was truthful.

Another assumption that people make is that if you have your own business in a large home, you must be independently wealthy. We were constantly asked by local groups and charities to donate rooms for a night or a weekend. At first we agreed to many of these requests and decided that we would cap these "freebies" at a yearly total of $1,000. We soon discovered that if people don't themselves pay for something, they won't take a reservation with you very seriously. We had people reserve and then cancel again and again. We had people who wanted to use their certificate for a one-night stay right in the middle of a holiday weekend. Generally, they would choose to stay on a Saturday night, which made it almost impossible to rent that room for the Friday or the Sunday nights, as most other guests wanted to stay for all three nights. It's also impossible to claim these free nights as a taxable charitable donation for your business income tax return. One needs to consider these requests very carefully.

One request that we did happily fulfill on several occasions was to host morning coffee for an area retirement home. When we were building the addition to our home, prior to opening the business, my father-in-law was a resident at this home. The centre took weekly outings in a large van. Every time they passed by our place, they would slow down and my father-in-law would proudly point out his son's place and tell everyone about the Bed and Breakfast we would be opening there soon. "They will have us all there for coffee when they open," he would tell everyone. Sadly, he passed away before we had finished the project.

One early spring day, we received a phone call from the activity organizer at the retirement home. "We were driving by your place the other day and the residents onboard the van all thought we were going to your place for morning coffee," she said. "When I told them that we weren't stopping with you, I had a small rebellion. Some people were even rapping their canes quite forcefully on the floor. I know your father-in-law is no longer with us, but do you think we could still come to you?" We readily agreed and a midweek morning was agreed upon.

We had not expected to be very busy with guests during this shoulder season but, of course, the night before their arrival, every room was full. We explained what was happening and the guests all thought it was a great idea. Everyone agreed to have breakfast at 8:00 a.m., and some even helped us restage the guest dining room and living room so that thirty elderly guests would all have a seat when they arrived at 10:00 a.m.

The seniors were absolutely delightful. They exclaimed over the table settings and one old dear told me very sadly, "You use your antique china every chance you get. One day you'll have to give it all away like I did." They lingered until lunchtime and for some, I think, naptime.

I offered to take the more mobile residents on a tour of the upstairs of the house. As we were climbing the stairs, a very young couple passed us going down the stairs. One of the women asked me in a very loud voice, "Norma, are those two married? I don't think they're married." I could hear the young couple chuckling as I gently explained that we weren't really supposed to ask that question when booking in guests.

***

When choosing a name for your business, many hosts will choose one that comes at the start of the alphabet. Potential guests have limited time for their online search and may not make it past the first three letters of the alphabet when looking for accommodation. In any reading that we did prior to opening the business, the recommendations regarding the choice of a name suggested that choosing too lengthy a name or one that is too "cutesy" has the potential to drive away some potential guests.

We found this to be particularly true with groups of golfers. Our area of Grey County offers a number of golf courses at different levels of playing difficulty. The cost to golf at these various courses is significantly lower than one would pay closer to big cities, so the area is a real destination for golfers.

Friends of ours who run a tour company offered to include our information in their booth at a travel and leisure show that took place in Toronto. They had stayed with us just after we opened the business and were quite taken with our place. They offered to help us out in this way, thinking this would be of benefit to our newly launched business. To their surprise, whenever they mentioned staying at a B&B to golfers attending the show, they got some real pushback. "We don't stay in frilly, chintzy places that smell like roses," one man told them. We found that this bias held true unless wives were accompanying their husbands on the weekend away.

In later years, we had some golfers tell us that they were quite surprised that they actually enjoyed staying with us and that they were quite relieved that the place didn't resemble an "old ladies' home." This was a continual surprise to us as our more contemporary rooms were quite clearly portrayed in our website photos.

Our business website was designed by a newly opened company located in Owen Sound. My reading on the topic had taught me that a website should be clear and concise. Potential guests don't want to read your whole life story. They want to know what you have to offer, what the cost is, what the place looks like, and if you have availability on the nights they need accommodation. You have less than a minute to capture their interest and "seal the deal."

After hosting our first wedding at the B&B, the professional wedding photographer offered to take photos of our home for our website. We eagerly took him up on his offer, not realizing that he also did the photos for local real estate agents. He presented us with over one hundred photos, each more beautiful than the one before. We were hard-pressed to select which photos we wanted to use.

Occasionally you'll still see a website where the owners have decided to use their own photos. Unless your other career is professional photography, I would strongly urge anyone thinking this is a good way to cut corners cost-wise to reconsider that decision.

People in the industry had warned us that the average lifespan of a B&B is five years. After that time, the owners simply wear out. Age could also be a factor in this, as a number of people go into the business after they retire from another career.

We hung in there for fifteen years, until knees needing replacing and other physical issues suggested that it was time to hang up our aprons.

People often ask us if we miss running a B&B. The answer is a resounding "Of course we do." We miss the people. We miss their laughter. We miss their excitement as they discover the beauty of the area in which they are staying. We miss the instant friendships and the opportunity to share a little of the lives of our many guests.

Over the years, hundreds of people from all over the world entered the doors of Holly Cottage and became part of the history of the house. The house truly does have a lot of stories to tell. I have told you only some of them.

Acknowledgements

I would like to acknowledge my husband, David, without whom there would not have been a Holly Cottage.

www.ingramcontent.com/pod-product-compliance
Lightning Source LLC
LaVergne TN
LVHW041545070426
835507LV00011B/944

9 781771 805421